Das Chinesische National-
museum in Peking
The National Museum of
China in Beijing

Meinhard von Gerkan
Stephan Schütz
Ma Lidong

Das Chinesische Nationalmuseum in Peking

The National Museum of China in Beijing

gmp · Architekten von Gerkan, Marg und Partner
CABR · China Academy of Building Research

Verortung	Location	8
Grußwort Lu Zhangshen	Opening Remarks Lu Zhangshen	12
Das Nationalmuseum als Symbol der Veränderung und Verständigung Martin Roth	The National Museum as a Symbol of Change and Reconciliation Martin Roth	16
Vorwort Meinhard von Gerkan	Preface Meinhard von Gerkan	18
Ein kultureller Handschlag: Der Bau des weltgrößten Museums András Szántó	A Cultural Handshake: Building the World's Largest Museum András Szántó	22
Eine deutsch-chinesische Zusammenarbeit Zhou Rong Ma Lidong Stephan Schütz	A German-Chinese Cooperation Zhou Rong Ma Lidong Stephan Schütz	38
Pläne und Zeichnungen	Plans and Drawings	50
Fotografische Dokumentation	Photographic Documentation	62
Anhang	Appendix	96

Verortung

39° 56' N, 116° 23' O

Location

THE NATIONAL MUSEUM OF CHINA Location

Peking Beijing

China

Shanghai

Peking

Der Stadtname bedeutet ins Deutsche übersetzt „Nördliche Hauptstadt", da ab der Ming-Dynastie die chinesischen Herrscher auch von Nanjing (Südliche Hauptstadt) aus das Land regierten. Während seiner 3000-jährigen Geschichte war Peking immer eines der politischen Zentren Chinas. Seit 1949 ist Peking die alleinige Hauptstadt der Volksrepublik China.

Peking ist mit einer Fläche von 16.808 km² so groß wie Schleswig-Holstein und hatte im Jahr 2012 über 20 Millionen. Konzentrisch breitet sich die Stadt von dem Kern der Verbotenen Stadt", dem alten Kaiserpalast, aus. Das Zentrum der Hauptstadt umfasst neben der „Verbotenen Stadt"[1] auch berühmte Einzelbauten wie zum Beispiel die Große Halle des Volkes[2] und das Nationalmuseum[3], die am Tiananmen Platz[4] liegen. Fünf Ringstraßen umgeben das Zentrum, an denen sich neue Stadtteilzentren entwickeln.

Neben seiner historischen und kulturellen Vorreiterrolle nimmt Peking auch eine Spitzenposition als Metropole der Industrie und Forschung ein.

Beijing

In English, the name Beijing means "Northern Capital". During the Ming Dynasty, the Chinese emperors ruled the country from two centers, namely Beijing and Nanjing, the "Southern Capital". Beijing has a 3,000-year history and has always been an important hub of Chinese politics and culture. Since 1949, Beijing has become the one and only capital of the People's Republic of China.

In 2012, Beijing had twenty million inhabitants and occupied a territory as large as 16,808 square kilometers—that is ten times the size of Greater London. The city is organized in a series of six concentric rings. The first ring is synonymous with the outer walls of the "Forbidden City,"[1] the former emperors' palace. In the vicinity of the palace, the city also includes a number of famous individual buildings such as the Great Hall of the People[2] and the National Museum of China.[3] They are all located around the world's largest public square, Tiananmen Square.[4] Five ring roads surround the historic center and individual city centers have been developing alongside.

Besides Beijing's historical and cultural importance, the Chinese capital is also gaining significance as a center for research and industry.

Peking in Zahlen
Fläche 16.808 km²,
Bevölkerung: 20,69 Mio. (Stand 2012)

Beijing in Figures
Area: 16,808 square kilometers,
Population: 20.69 million

THE NATIONAL MUSEUM OF CHINA Location Detail

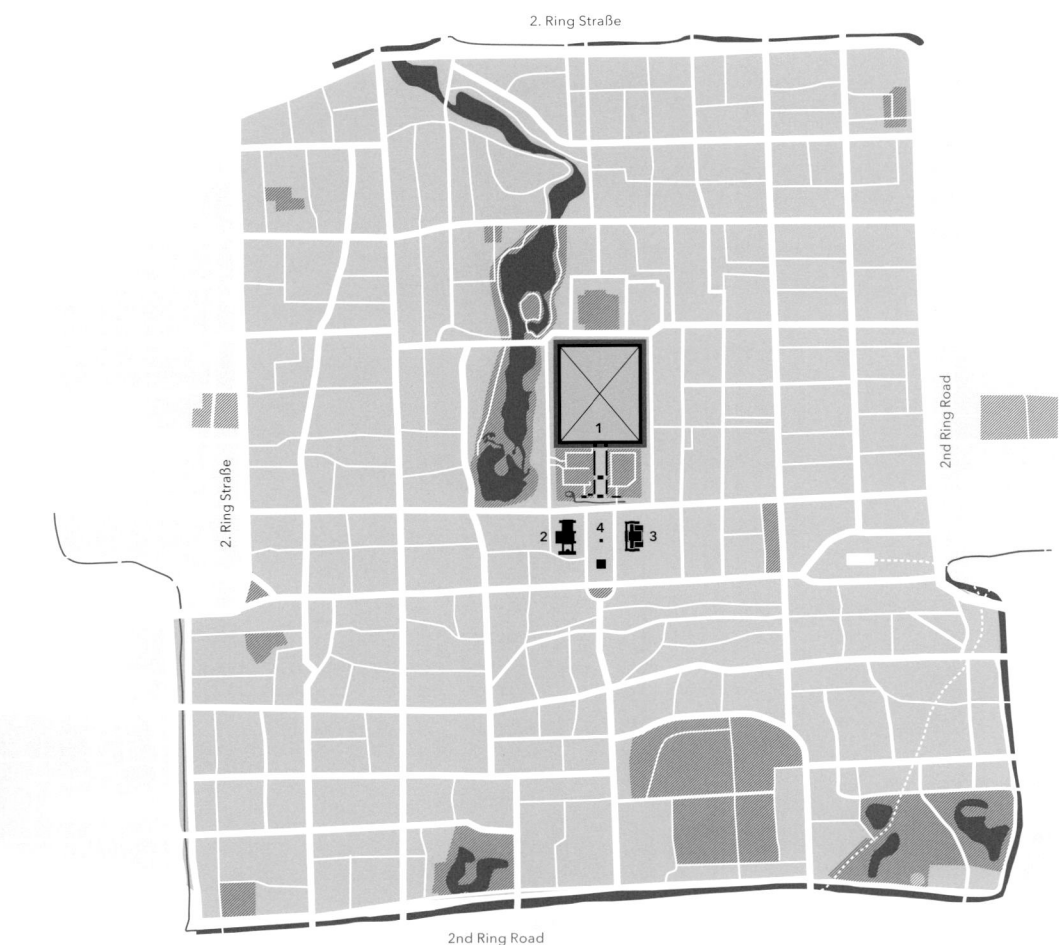

Peking Innenstadt
Beijing Inner City

Wasserstraßen
Waterways
Grünflächen
Greens
Verkehrswege
Traffic Routes

Grußwort

Lu Zhangshen – Direktor des Chinesischen
Nationalmuseums, Peking

Seit seiner Fertigstellung vor über zwei Jahren zieht das Chinesische Nationalmuseum Besucher an wie ein Magnet. Die Marke von zehn Millionen wurde bereits überschritten. Diese zweifellos beeindruckende Besuchermenge setzt sich aus allen Bereichen des chinesischen Volkes, ausländischen Touristen sowie politisch Verantwortlichen aus dem In- und Ausland zusammen. Selbstverständlich übt das Museum auch eine große Anziehung auf Wissenschaftler und Experten aus verschiedenen Fachbereichen und Nationen aus. Weiterhin erfahren wir aus all diesen Kreisen großes Interesse und Lob hinsichtlich der architektonischen Neugestaltung und Erweiterung des Chinesischen Nationalmuseums. Das internationale Echo unter den Besuchern, Fachleuten sowie in den Medien fällt durchweg positiv aus. Insbesondere die Verzahnung von alter Substanz mit neuer zeitgemäßer Architektur wird als besonders gelungen empfunden. Die Wertschätzung bezieht sich sowohl auf das innere wie auch auf das äußere Erscheinungsbild des Museums einschließlich seiner Eingliederung in das städtebauliche Umfeld. Somit kann man in jeder Hinsicht sagen, dass der Entwurf und die Ausführung die funktionalen und gestalterischen Anforderungen vollauf erfüllt haben. Dabei war es im Fall des Chinesischen Nationalmuseums ungemein schwierig, in allen Fragen einen gemeinsamen Nenner zu finden. In meiner Rolle als Vertreter des Bauherrn fühlte ich mich zu jeder Zeit von den beteiligten Architekten voll verstanden und gewürdigt, was ich als außerordentlich ehrenhaft begreife.

Der architektonische Entwurf – und folgerichtig der Erfolg des neuen Nationalmuseums – entstammt der Kooperation zwischen gmp Architekten aus Deutschland und der China Academy of Building Research (CABR). Diese erfolgreiche Zusammenarbeit ist einer der wichtigsten Faktoren für die großartige Resonanz, die das Museum überall auf der Welt erfahren hat. Ich bedanke mich hiermit sehr herzlich für den Einsatz, die Bemühungen und die hervorragende Zusammenarbeit des Entwurfsteams.

Insbesondere drei wesentliche Punkte habe ich seit der erfolgreichen Fertigstellung des Museums verinnerlicht: Erstens: Was sollte man tun, wenn der Bauherr mit dem Entwurf des ersten Preisträgers eines Architekturwettbewerbs nicht ganz zufrieden ist oder wenn der Entwurf die Erfordernisse nicht vollständig erfüllt? Als Fazit mag gelten, dass der Entwurf überarbeitet werden sollte, bis eine allgemeine Zufriedenheit entsteht. Diesem positiven Endresultat geht ein Prozess der intensiven Auseinandersetzung und Verständigung zwischen Bauherr und Architekt voraus. In der Regel ist das leichter gesagt als getan. Aber im Fall der Entwurfsüberarbeitung für das Nationalmuseum gelang dies zur beiderseitigen Zufriedenheit auf eine äußerst kooperative Art und Weise.

Zweitens: Das Entwurfsteam sollte hoch motiviert sein, den Entwurf immer weiter zu verbessern. Grundvoraussetzung dafür ist, dass die Planungsbüros erfahrene und ehrgeizige Mitarbeiter mit dem Projekt betrauen. Dies zu bewerkstelligen, gelang beiden Partnerbüros. Dabei bin ich persönlich besonders Herrn Stephan Schütz, Partner von gmp Architekten, und Herrn Ma Lidong, Vertreter des chinesischen Partnerbüros, dankbar. Beide Herren brachten ihre hoch professionellen und kreativen Fähigkeiten in unsere gemeinsame Zusammenarbeit ein. Innerhalb kürzester Zeit schafften sie es, den Entwurf so zu optimieren, dass er auf breite Zustimmung stieß. Das stellte einen entscheidenden Meilenstein auf dem Weg zu dem großen Projekterfolg des Chinesischen Nationalmuseums dar.

Drittens: Der Bauherr sollte zu allen Zeiten des Projekts auch über architektonisches Fachwissen und einen Begriff von dessen baulicher Umsetzung verfügen. Denn es kann und darf nicht sein, dass der Bauherr aufgrund seines Kompetenzmangels die Arbeit des Architekten unzureichend begleitet, was zu irritierenden oder unrealisierbaren Änderungen des Entwurfs führen kann. Dieser Punkt ist von ungeheurer Wichtigkeit, da er, falls nicht beachtet, massiven Mehraufwand und Verzögerungen auslösen kann.

Opening Remarks

Lu Zhangshen – Museum Director of the
Chinese National Museum, Beijing

Since its completion over two years ago, the Chinese National Museum has been a magnet for large numbers of visitors. Well over ten million visitors have entered the museum and filled its galleries so far. This impressive number includes people from all over China, international tourists, as well as politicians and diplomats from China and abroad. The museum also exerts an enormous fascination on scientists and experts from a variety of fields and nationalities. As a result, we have received a great deal of public support and praise regarding the architectural redesign and extension of the Chinese National Museum. The international feedback from visitors, experts, and the media has been entirely positive. In particular, the combination of historical elements with contemporary architecture has been regarded as very successful. There has been unanimous praise for the urban integration, as well as the museum's interior and exterior design. We are proud that the design and its implementation fulfill all aspects of our functional and aesthetic aims. Given the myriad requirements and expectations, it proved especially difficult to find a common consensus during the design process. However, in my role as the client's representative, I always received both architects' full support and appreciation. I have felt very honored by this.

The architectural design – and therefore the success of the refurbished Chinese National Museum – originated from the cooperation between gmp Architects from Germany and the China Academy of Building Research (CABR). This positive collaboration was an important reason for the tremendous response we have had from all over the world. I express my sincere thanks to the design team for their continued effort and superb teamwork.

Since the successful completion of the Chinese National Museum I have taken three essential elements to heart: Firstly, what can be done if the client is not completely happy with the winning architect's design? The only solution lies in achieving a common consensus as quickly as possible. Any solution of that kind is usually developed through a laborious and intense exchange between client and architect; however, this is easier said than done. Nevertheless, in the case of the Chinese National Museum we achieved this through an admirable degree of close cooperation.

Secondly, the design team needs to be highly motivated to improve the design continuously. Experienced and ambitious individuals play a very important role in this process. Both architectural practices succeeded in doing so. I am personally grateful to Stephan Schütz, partner at gmp architects, and Ma Lidong from the China Academy of Building Research. These two gentlemen contributed to the project's success with their highly professional and creative abilities. Within a short period of time, they succeeded in improving the design to such a degree that in the end it received broad support. This was an essential milestone on the road to success.

Thirdly, at all times a client needs to have some architectural knowledge and an understanding of how to turn design into built reality. It is vital that a client should not obstruct the architectural design due to his lack of understanding. This item is of greatest importance, as it will inevitably lead to enormous costs and delays.

Im August 2013 eröffneten gmp Architekten, die für den Entwurf des Chinesischen Nationalmuseums federführenden Architekten aus Deutschland, im Museum selbst eine Ausstellung über ihre Arbeit am Nationalmuseum und eine allgemeine Werkschau ihrer Architektur der breiten Öffentlichkeit zeigen. Ich möchte an dieser Stelle gmp Architekten meine persönlichen Glückwünsche übermitteln. Es war mir eine Ehre, dass wir als Bauherren über dieses Projekt gmp Architekten und das China Academy of Building Research kennenlernen und mit den professionellen Teams beider Büros zusammenarbeiten konnten. Dank dieser inspirierenden Teamarbeit, dank der kooperativen Arbeitseinstellung und der starken Kreativität, gelang es beiden Architekturbüros, den Entwurf des Chinesischen Nationalmuseums so erfolgreich zu realisieren. Sie setzten damit ein herausragendes Zeichen für die Erweiterung und Neugestaltung eines derart prestigeträchtigen Bauwerks.

In August 2013, gmp Architects, who have been the lead architects in designing the Chinese National Museum, installed an exhibition in the Museum itself which shows gmp's design for the museum and other international gmp projects. I would like to take this opportunity to personally congratulate gmp Architects on their successful work. It has been an honor for me that I, as the client representative, had the pleasure of working both with gmp and the China Academy of Building Research. Thanks to their inspiring cooperation, both teams managed to successfully complete the design of the Chinese National Museum. It has become a widely recognized symbol of the refurbishment of a prestigious national monument.

Das Nationalmuseum als Symbol der Veränderung und Verständigung

Martin Roth – Direktor des Victoria and Albert Museum in London

Nur wenn sich die Zeitläufte in solcher Geschwindigkeit verändern, dass man schon nach wenigen Jahren Vorgänge als Geschichte betrachtet, merkt man, dass eine radikale Umwälzung stattgefunden hat. Aus der heutigen Sicht erscheint es nichts Ungewöhnliches zu sein, in China zu arbeiten, Bauvorhaben in erheblichem Ausmaße zu realisieren oder sich kulturell zu engagieren, das heißt, sich auch auf einen mehr oder minder unmittelbaren Diskurs einzulassen.

Vor 15 Jahren war, was heute Alltag ist, undenkbar. Die Zeiten – und damit die Bedingungen – haben sich rasant geändert, China hat sich geöffnet und wir sind Teil dieses Öffnungsprozesses, auch weil unsere Wirtschaft aufs engste mit China verwoben ist.

Pionierleistungen wie der Um- und Neubau des Chinesischen Nationalmuseums sind nicht nur Bestandteil dieses Öffnungsprozesses, sondern ein Katalysator und Beschleuniger desselben. Das Museum in Peking ist ein Symbol der Veränderung und Verständigung, ein Zeichen nationalen Bewusstseins und Stolzes einerseits und gleichzeitiger Öffnung andererseits, ein Widerspruch in sich, eine architektonische Quadratur des politischen Kreises, der je nach Blickrichtung unterschiedlich wahrgenommen wird. Aus meiner Sicht sind die Architekten von Gerkan, Marg und Partner (gmp) meisterliche Diplomaten ihres Fachs, Übersetzer unterschiedlichster Werkethik und Bewusstseinserweiterer für China und Deutschland. Es ist gmp und anderen Büros zu danken, dass sie mit ihren internationalen Teams neue Dimensionen nicht nur in die chinesische Architektur, sondern auch in das Alltagsverständnis eingeführt haben.

Keine Frage, das NMC ist maßstabslos – in jeglicher Hinsicht: Der Bau erreicht Größenordnungen, die für europäische Verhältnisse nicht nachzuvollziehen sind. Ich hatte die Chance, die Planungen seit spätestens 2000 zu verfolgen und für lange Zeit zu begleiten. Vom verstaubten und sanierungsbedürftigen Museum, voll von Kopien und Kuriosa, bis hin zum Nationalmuseum in neuem Glanz liegen nur wenige Jahre. Es ist ein Museum entstanden, das jedem Standard weltweit standhalten kann.

Es wird vermutlich noch lange dauern, bis die Geschichtsschreibung Chinas objektiviert dargestellt werden kann. Es werden aber in diesem Museum Versuche zur Geschichtsdefinition unternommen, etwa über die Ausstellung zur „Kunst der Aufklärung", eine jener Ausstellungen, die mich mit dem Nationalmuseum verbinden.

Die Beauftragung der Architekten von Gerkan, Marg und Partner (gmp) und deren lokalem Planungspartner China Academy of Building Research (CABR), das Nationalmuseum Chinas zu entwerfen, zu planen und zu bauen, zeigt, dass die Suche nach einer neuen chinesischen Identität längst kein Prozess mehr ist, der unter Ausschluss der Weltöffentlichkeit stattfindet. Die Architekten leisten ihren Beitrag zu diesem Prozess.

The National Museum as a Symbol of Change and Reconciliation

Martin Roth – Director of the Victoria and Albert Museum in London

When times change at such speed that processes are viewed as history only a few years after they have occurred, it becomes clear that radical changes have taken place. From today's perspective, it does not seem extraordinary to work in China, to complete a substantial number of construction projects, and to engage in cultural exchanges – in other words, to embark on a more or less direct discourse. What is now an everyday scenario was unthinkable fifteen years ago. The times – and hence the conditions – have changed very rapidly. China has opened up and we are part of that process, not least because our economy is closely interwoven with that of China.

Pioneering efforts such as the conversion and new construction of the National Museum in Beijing are not only part of this process of opening up, but a catalyst and accelerator for it. The National Museum is a symbol of change and reconciliation.

It is a sign of national awareness and pride on the one hand and of openness on the other – a contradiction in itself, an architectural squaring of the political circle which can be perceived in different ways depending on one's position. From my perspective, the architects von Gerkan, Marg and Partners are expert diplomats in their field, translators of very diverse work ethics and capable of stretching people's minds in both China and Germany. It is thanks to gmp, and other practices and their international teams, that new dimensions have been introduced to Chinese architecture, and common perceptions have been broadened.

There is no doubt that the Chinese National Museum is off the scale in every respect. A building of such size and dimension cannot be imagined in a European setting. I have been able to watch the design process from the year 2000, and to follow it firsthand for a long time. Only a few years separate the old museum – a dusty place in need of an overhaul, full of replicas and curiosities – from the current National Museum in its splendid new form. A world-class museum has been created.

It will probably take a long time before China's history can be recorded objectively. But attempts to define history are taking place in this museum, for example in the "Art of the Enlightenment" exhibition – an exhibition that forms part of my own history of collaboration with the National Museum.

The fact that the architects von Gerkan, Marg and Partners (gmp) and their local design partners, the China Academy for Building Research (CABR) were commissioned to design, plan, and build the Chinese National Museum, indicates that the search for a new Chinese identity is no longer a process happening behind closed national doors, but one that is taking place on the world stage. The architects von Gerkan, Marg and Partners are making their contribution to this process.

Vorwort

Meinhard von Gerkan

Meine erste Begegnung mit China fand statt, als unser Architekturbüro gmp 1998 zum Wettbewerb für den Neubau der Deutschen Schule nach Peking eingeladen wurde.

Der Besuch der Verbotenen Stadt, der Ausflug zur Chinesischen Mauer – das hat mich nachhaltig beeindruckt. Unter den Kollegen haben wir dann Wetten abgeschlossen, wann die Schule fertig sein würde. Wir gewannen den Wettbewerb und der Bau wurde in einer eminent kurzen Zeit realisiert – weshalb ich meine Wette verlor.

Das Potenzial Chinas war damals für mich überhaupt nicht erkennbar. Ich bin nach China gefahren und musste feststellen, dass meine Vorstellung von diesem Land als einem Entwicklungsland ziemlich falsch war: Es gab nahezu alles zu kaufen, es waren mehr Autos und weit weniger Fahrräder unterwegs als ich dachte, die Hotels boten europäischen Standard, die Restaurants zum Teil vorzügliche Qualität. Es gab viel zur Schau gestellten Reichtum und Luxus. Das Land war viel weiter entwickelt, als ich erwartet hatte. Dass China ein Zukunftsmarkt für Architektur und Städtebau werden würde, dieser Gedanke war zum Zeitpunkt meiner ersten Chinareise überhaupt nicht präsent.

Die entscheidende Wende war, knapp zwei Jahre später, ein Zufallsereignis. In Peking fand im Sommer 1999 der UIA-Kongress – das Welttreffen der Architekten – statt. Ich war zu einem Vortrag eingeladen und wir erhielten die Chance, in einem renommierten Museum eine Ausstellung unserer Architektur zu realisieren. Die Ausstellung war ein großer Erfolg, auch in den Medien, nicht zuletzt durch die guten Kontakte der Gastgeberin zu maßgeblichen Leuten aus Politik und Kultur. Zuvor hatte es in Peking noch nie eine Architekturausstellung in einem Museum gegeben. Das war so etwas wie eine Explosion in Sachen Öffentlichkeitsarbeit. Wir konnten uns in der Folge einen Ruf als erfolgreiche und zuverlässige Architekten aufbauen.

Lange dominierten in China Bilder amerikanischer Architektur, verbunden mit dekorativen Elementen aus der chinesischen Tradition, die meistens zur Karikatur ihrer selbst mutierten.

Wir vertraten unbeirrt unsere eigene Position: sachlich, einfach, reduziert in den Materialien, konstruktionsbetont und funktional logisch, sowie mit natürlichen Eigenschaften, energiesparend und optimalen Tageslichtbedingungen. Zunächst erwarteten wir, hiermit bestenfalls eine Außenseiterposition zu besetzen. Die heute, nach zwölf Jahren nahezu fast dominierende „chinoise Sachlichkeit" hat unsere Architekturauffassung in eine Vorbildfunktion gebracht und uns in weit über 200 Wettbewerben ein beachtlich großes Auftragsvolumen eingetragen, auch in Konkurrenz zu amerikanischen Kollegen.

Das Einzige, was letztendlich Bestand haben wird, ist eine Architektur, die sich nachhaltig und dauerhaft aus den Bedingungen, aus dem sozialen Kontext, aus der Funktion, aus der Rücksicht gegenüber dem städtischen Kontext, sofern noch vorhanden, aus der Ökonomie und letztlich aus einer zeitlosen Gestaltungsabsicht generiert.

Beim Nationalmuseum waren die Transformation traditioneller Elemente der chinesischen Kultur und die kontrastierende Kombination mit unserer puristisch-einfachen Formensprache der wichtigste Teil unserer Arbeit. Unsere Auffassung bestätigt sich in der These, dass nur konträre Spannung den Fortschritt der Baukultur befördert, nicht jedoch Nachahmung und Anpassung. Es war unser wichtigstes Ziel, die Symbiose von Alt und Neu in eine Balance zu bringen.

Neben den kulturellen und sprachlichen Unterschieden zwischen Europäern und Chinesen gibt es natürlich auch große Unterschiede in der Mentalität und in der Art der Kommunikation und der Kooperation. Wir Westeuropäer, speziell wir Deutschen, müssen bei unseren Aktivitäten in China lernen, geduldig zu sein und nicht allzu zielgerichtet auf schnelle Entscheidungen zu drängen. Wir haben gelernt, dass ein höflicher Chinese niemals definitiv „nein" sagt, und haben verstanden, dass manchmal das Wort „vielleicht" schon so viel wie „nein" bedeuten kann. Auch, dass Gesichtsverlust für einen Chinesen eine große Schmach bedeutet und deswegen jedes Verhalten darauf ausgerichtet sein muss, dies möglichst zu vermeiden, für den Verhandlungspartner gleichermaßen wie für uns selbst. Wir, die wir es gewohnt sind, sehr gradlinig und ohne Umschweife unsere Meinung zu sagen, sind in dieser Hinsicht lernbedürftig.

Preface

Meinhard von Gerkan

I had my first encounter with China when, in 1998, our architectural practice, gmp, was invited to take part in the competition for the new construction of the German School in Beijing.

The visit to the Forbidden City and the excursion to the Great Wall of China—these left a lasting impression on me. We took bets between colleagues as to when the school would be completed. We won the competition, and the building was completed in an extremely short time—and I lost my bet.

At that time, I completely failed to appreciate China's potential. When I traveled to China I had to recognize that my idea of this country as a developing country was rather mistaken: you could buy nearly everything, there were many more cars and less bicycles on the roads than I had anticipated, the hotels offered European standards, and some of the restaurants were of an excellent quality. There was much ostentatious wealth and luxury. The country was much more developed than I had anticipated. That China would become a future market for architecture and urban design was a thought that, at the time of my first trip to China, was completely absent.

The important change, barely two years later, was the result of an accidental event. In the summer of 1999, Beijing hosted the UIA Congress—the world meeting for architects. I had been invited to give a lecture and we were given the opportunity to stage an exhibition of our architecture in a well-known museum. The exhibition was a great success, also in the media, not least due to the host's excellent contacts with important personalities in politics and culture. Up to that date, there had never been an architectural exhibition in a museum in Beijing. There was something of an explosion in terms of public relations. As a result, we were able to build up a reputation as successful and reliable architects.

For a long time, developments in China had been dominated by American architecture combined with decorative elements from the Chinese tradition, which often ended up as a caricature of itself.

We were unfazed and insisted on our own position: rational, simple, reduced choice of materials, with an emphasis on the construction and functional logic, with natural properties, energy-saving and optimum daylight conditions. Initially we only expected to be afforded the position of a outsider, at best. Today, after twelve years, the "chinoise Sachlichkeit" (Chinese rational style)—which is close to dominating Chinese architectural style—has elevated our architectural approach to an exemplary level and, in well over 200 competitions, has earned us a substantial volume of commissions, also in competition with American colleagues.

What will ultimately prevail is an architecture that is generated sustainably and durably based on the actual conditions, the social context, the functional requirements, an understanding of the urban context (where this is still available), on the commercial requirements, and finally also on a timeless design intent.

At the National Museum, the transformation of traditional elements of Chinese culture and the contrasting combination with our purist/simple pattern language was the most important part of our work. Nevertheless, our belief that progress in architecture evolves from contrasting tension rather than from imitation and adaptation was confirmed. Our most important objective was to achieve a balance in the symbiosis of the old and new. Obviously, there are enormous differences between Europeans and the Chinese, not only in terms of culture and language, but also with respect to mentality and the method of communication and cooperation. Western Europeans, particularly we Germans, have to learn to be patient when working in China and to not be too focused on pushing for quick decisions. We have learned that a polite Chinese will never reply with a definite "no", and we have understood that sometimes the word "perhaps" may already mean as much as "no". We have also learned that loss of face is a serious issue for any Chinese and that therefore one has to strive to avoid this at all costs, both for oneself as much as for one's partner in the negotiation. For us, who are used to offering our opinions in a very straightforward and direct way, this required a fairly steep learning curve.

Was ich als sehr angenehm empfinde, ist eine Art von Ritualisierung des Lebens. Dinge passieren nicht alle nur im Schnelldurchgang, sondern man nimmt sich Zeit. Wir haben es daher zu schätzen gelernt, dass geschäftliche Besprechungen und Vertragsverhandlungen immer wieder von gesellschaftlichen Aktivitäten wie einem gemeinsamen Essen und Toastsprüchen begleitet werden, was den menschlichen Austausch und das Zusammensein angenehm macht. Unterhaltungen werden auch in Metaphern geführt. So ein metaphorisches Gespräch hat ein sehr angenehmes Niveau, ist aber auf gewisse Weise zweideutig. Was uns allerdings nach wie vor schwer fällt, ist, die raffinierte Taktik des Verhandelns zu verstehen und selbst zu beherrschen. Immer wieder fühlen wir uns in dieser Hinsicht unterlegen.

Beeindruckend finde ich die Dynamik, die Schnelligkeit und in einem gewissen Sinne die Offenheit gegenüber Neuem, die Begierde, neue Dinge zu wagen und zu realisieren – und das verbunden mit überaus schnellen Entscheidungsprozessen. Was in Deutschland wie eine Schnecke dahinkriecht, vollzieht sich in China in einem atemberaubenden Tempo.

Konfliktlösungen im interkulturellen Dialog

› Der Entwurfsprozess per Dialog ist manchmal ein steiniger Weg. Er ist oftmals mit weitgehenden und sehr nachhaltigen Meinungsverschiedenheiten und gegenseitiger Überzeugungsarbeit verbunden, namentlich dort, wo es aufgrund kultureller Unterschiede zu Differenzen zwischen Bauherren und Planern kommt. China hat einen Großteil seiner 5000-jährigen Kulturgeschichte in dem großen Museum versammelt, das zur Mao-Zeit am Tiananmen-Platz direkt neben der Verbotenen Stadt errichtet wurde. Wegen seines maroden Bauzustands, seines sehr düsteren und für die Öffentlichkeit wenig attraktiven Charakters sollte dieses Gebäude komplett umgestaltet werden; zu diesem Zweck wurde ein internationaler Wettbewerb zwischen einer beschränkten Zahl namhafter Architekten ausgelobt.

Unser Wettbewerbsentwurf sah im Gegensatz zu dem damals noch vorhandenen Bau aus der Mao-Zeit eine große Ausstellungsfläche – 30 Prozent der gesamten Ausstellungskapazität – in einem voluminösen Dachgeschoss vor, das über einer Grand Hall angeordnet war und über lange Rolltreppen erreicht werden konnte. Wir planten, das Dach mit poliertem Kupfer zu verkleiden und einer weit auskragenden Attika zu versehen. Die Besonderheit dieses Entwurfs bestand darin, dass die Besucher von diesem großen, hochgelegenen Ausstellungsgeschoss Blickkontakt sowohl zum Tiananmen-Platz als auch zur Verbotenen Stadt und den anderen an diesem Ort versammelten wichtigsten Repräsentativbauten Chinas aufnehmen konnten.

Zunächst verlief der Planungsprozess relativ einvernehmlich. Je mehr allerdings der Entwurf sich konkretisierte, desto lauter machten sich Stimmen bemerkbar, die unsere Konzeption zu neuzeitlich fanden. Das von uns geplante Gebäude beeinträchtige die Einheit und Harmonie des historischen Gebäude-Ensembles um den Tiananmen-Platz, insbesondere störe die Ausbildung des Daches. Aus dieser Kritik entspann sich ein langer, komplizierter und vielstimmiger Dialog, mit dem Ergebnis, dass man uns zunächst von der weiteren Bearbeitung des Projektes suspendierte, es sei denn, wir wären bereit, auf kritische Anmerkungen von chinesischer Seite Rücksicht zu nehmen und uns darum zu bemühen, dass vor allem die Kontinuität der Dachattiken gewahrt bleibe, die eine lange chinesische Tradition aufweisen und in der Tat zu den prägnantesten Elementen chinesischer Architektur gehören.

Daraus ergaben sich nach langen Diskussionen innerhalb unseres Büros eine Reihe modifizierter Entwürfe, die zu guter Letzt auf das Ausstellungsgeschoss im Dach verzichteten und sich äußerlich, speziell in der Ausbildung der Dachattika mit zurückgestaffelten Auskragungen, an die anderen Bauten anpassten. Gleichermaßen durften wir das Innere des Museums in einer sehr zeitgemäßen, strengen, geradlinigen und vor allem großzügigen Raumfolge gestalten.

Das mittlerweile eröffnete Museum ist das Ergebnis eines gelungenen Kompromisses aus Alt und Neu, aus traditioneller chinesischer und moderner internationaler Architektur, wobei die letztgenannte die heimische Kultur harmonisch integriert.

What I also find very appealing is a kind of ritualization of life. Not everything has to happen at top speed; instead, people take their time. We have therefore learned to appreciate that business meetings and contract negotiations often take place in the context of social activities such as a shared meal and toast speeches, which makes for pleasant human exchange and togetherness. Conversations are often cloaked in metaphors. Such metaphoric exchanges take place at a very agreeable level, although they may in some way be somewhat ambiguous. What we still struggle with, however, is understanding and mastering the clever methods of negotiating. Time and again, we feel less capable in this respect.

I am very impressed with the dynamism, the speed and, in a certain sense, the openness towards new approaches, the desire to try something new and to implement it—and that combined with really fast decision processes. What in Germany progresses at a snail's pace takes place at breathtaking speed in China.

Conflict Resolution via Inter-cultural Dialogue

› The design process involving dialogue can be a stony path. It is often associated with very extensive and persistent differences of opinion and the need to persuade each other, especially in situations where differences occur between client and designer due to cultural differences.

China has collected many artifacts relating to its 5,000 years of cultural history in the large museum, which was built during Mao's time at Tiananmen Square, directly adjacent to the Forbidden City. Because of its poor structural condition and its very dark and — for the public — rather uninviting character, this building was to make way for a new building for which an international competition had been organized among a limited number of well-known architects.

In contrast to the building dating from the Mao era, our competition entry included a large exhibition space—30% of the total exhibition capacity—in a voluminous attic floor, which was situated above a Grand Hall and could be reached via long escalators. We had planned to clad the roof with polished copper and include a far-protruding parapet. The special feature of this design was that visitors who ventured up to this large, elevated exhibition floor were offered a view of both Tiananmen Square and of the Forbidden City, as well as the vicinity's other very important representational buildings.

Initially, the design process proceeded in relative agreement with the state officials in charge of the project. However, as our design proceeded to take more detailed shape, more and more opinions could be heard that felt that our concept was too contemporary. The view was that the building planned by us was detrimental to the unity and harmony of the historic building ensemble around Tiananmen Square, particularly the design of the roof. This criticism led to a long-drawn-out, complicated dialogue with many voices, with the result that we would be suspended from further work on the project unless we were prepared to take into account critical comments from the Chinese side and make an effort to retain, above all, the uniformity of the roof parapets, which were considered to be part of a long Chinese tradition and which, in fact, are one of the most conspicuous architectural elements in China.

In turn this led—after long discussions within the practice—to a series of modified designs that finally omitted the exhibition floor in the roof and were externally more adapted to the other buildings, particularly with respect to the design of the roof parapet with staggered, receding projections. In turn, we were allowed to design the interior of the museum in a very contemporary, austere, and straight-lined style, which, most importantly, included a generous sequence of spaces.

The museum, which has now been opened, is the result of a successful compromise between old and new, between traditional Chinese and modern international architecture, with the latter deferentially fitting in with the local culture.

Ein kultureller Handschlag:
Der Bau des weltgrößten Museums

Eine Architekturkritik von András Szántó

Museen sind bleibende Symbole der Errungenschaften und Visionen eines Landes. Von Katar über Brasilien bis nach Indien: Überall errichten aufstrebende Nationen Bauten für die Künste, nicht selten unter Mitwirkung internationaler Architekten. Nirgends findet diese Entwicklung einen größeren Niederschlag als in China, wo der Staat im Jahr circa 100 neue Museen in Auftrag gibt – 1000 neue Kunsteinrichtungen in einem Jahrzehnt! Jede chinesische Provinz und Stadt, so scheint es, hat ein eigenes Projekt in Arbeit. Viele dieser Bauten sind vitaler Bestandteil nicht nur großer Bauprojekte, sondern auch eines gewaltigen Investitionszyklus in öffentliche Infrastruktur und in kulturelle „soft power".

1

Der Entwurf des neuen Chinesischen Nationalmuseums im Zentrum von Peking ist wohl das symbolträchtigste all dieser Kulturprojekte. Es ist nicht umsonst Chinas führendes Museum; es ist der Ort, an dem ein Land von 1,4 Milliarden Einwohnern seine Geschichte der eigenen Bevölkerung und der restlichen Welt vermittelt. Das Nationalmuseum wurde 2011 nach Plänen des deutschen Architekturbüro von Gerkan, Marg und Partner (gmp) in Zusammenarbeit mit dem örtlichen Design-Institut China Academy of Building Research (CABR) fertiggestellt. Präsentiert wird zum einen die 5000-jährige Geschichte der chinesischen Zivilisation, zum anderen vermitteln Einzelausstellungen Aspekte internationaler Kultur. Es ist ein globales Museum für ein global vernetztes China – und das musste in der Architektur zum Ausdruck kommen.

Im Einklang mit diesen Ansprüchen lässt der Entwurf vielfältige Assoziationen entstehen. Für den Bauherrn war die eindeutige Verbindung zur chinesischen Kultur und Geschichte jedoch am wichtigsten. Die Lage des Museums unterstrich den Wunsch nach Kontextualisierung: Das Nationalmuseum sollte einen historischen Bau beziehen, der auf die Gründerzeit der Volksrepublik China zurückverweist – und bereits selbst eine stolze Museumstradition aufzuweisen hatte. Eine entsprechende Umnutzung, so glaubte der chinesische Bauherr, würde einen organischeren Dialog mit dem städtischen Umfeld ermöglichen als manch anderes von westlichen Architekten erst kürzlich errichtete Projekt. So zeichenhaft und innovativ diese neuen Bauten auch sein mögen, vielfach zeigen sie der Stadt und deren gewachsener Struktur die kalte Schulter.

Das neue Nationalmuseum sollte nicht nur etwas über China aussagen, sondern ebenso über Chinas Platz in der Welt. Darauf antworteten die Architekten mit einer feinen Balance aus chinesischen und westlichen Gestaltungsmerkmalen. Sie kombinierten das auf Understatement setzende Vokabular der internationalen Architekturmoderne mit deutlichen Verweisen auf die chinesische Kulturtradition. Der Entwurf verkörpert die unmissverständliche Botschaft, dass sich die Geschichte und die Geschichten von Chinas kultureller Evolution erneut an die Außenwelt binden. Die Transformation des historischen Gebäudes in ein modernes Museum symbolisiert gleichsam die außergewöhnliche Neuausrichtung von Chinas Identität und Selbstbild.

› Direkt am Tiananmen-Platz[1] (Platz des himmlischen Friedens) gelegen, dem historischen, kulturellen und politischen Dreh- und Angelpunkt Chinas, nur einige

A Cultural Handshake: Building the World's Largest Museum

An Architectural Criticism by András Szántó

Museums are enduring emblems of a country's achievements and aspirations. From Qatar to Brazil to India, ascendant nations everywhere are building new art institutions, often with international architects. Nowhere is the trend more apparent than in China, where state policy has mandated the construction of one hundred museums a year — a staggering one thousand new institutions over a decade. Each province and city, it seems, has a project in the works. The buildings, many of them anchoring vast development schemes, are part of an epochal cycle of investment into public infrastructure and soft power.

The design of the new National Museum of China, situated in the heart of Beijing, is freighted with more symbolism than most. This, after all, is China's ranking museum — the place where a country of 1.4 billion tells its story to its citizens and to the world. Completed in 2011 by the German architectural firm of von Gerkan, Marg und Partner (gmp), in collaboration with local design partner CABR China Academy for Building Research, the museum showcases 5,000 years of Chinese civilization, along with exhibitions that introduce Chinese citizens to facets of international culture. It is a global museum for a globally connected China — and the architecture needed to reflect that.

The National Museum's design invokes a multitude of bridging and linking themes to serve these aspirations. Most important for the commissioning authorities, the building had to express a clear connection to Chinese culture and history. The site underscored the desire for a contextual approach. The National Museum, it was decided, would inhabit a historic structure dating back to the foundational period of the People's Republic — a building that already had a well-established legacy as a museum. Adaptive reuse, the Chinese clients believed, would ensure a more organic dialogue with the surroundings than is evidenced in many recent projects in Beijing by Western architects. Iconic and innovative as those buildings are, they appear to turn their backs, by and large, on their host environment.

The new museum would have to say something not only about China, but also about China's place in the world. The architects responded with a carefully calibrated balance of Chinese and Western design attitudes. They combined the understated vocabulary of international architectural modernism with ever-present allusions to Chinese cultural traditions. The design sends an unmistakable signal that China's evolutionary narrative is now once again tied to the outside world. The building's transformation has mapped onto China's emblematic museum the extraordinary realignment in the country's identity and self-image.

› Overlooking Tiananmen Square,[1] the historic, cultural, and political fulcrum of China, steps from Chairman Mao's mausoleum and the gate to the Forbidden City, the columned edifice of the National Museum originated as one of the Shi Da Jianzhu, or "Ten Great Buildings," hastily erected in 1959 to mark the tenth anniversary of the People's Republic. Construction of the original structure, based on Soviet classicist plans by Tsinghua University and the Beijing Architectural Design Institute (BIAD), with Zhang Kaiji in the role of lead architect, took just ten months. Through much of its life, the structure housed not one but two museums, one dedicated to Chinese history, the other to the Chinese revolution. The precursor to the former was the Preparatory Office of the National History Museum, created in the summer of 1912 — the first museum operated by the Chinese government. It was physically located, from 1912, at the Imperial College, and later moved to the Forbidden City. In 1949, it was renamed the Beijing National History Museum to mark the founding of the People's Republic; its name changed again in 1959, to the National Museum of Chinese History. The predecessor of the Museum of Chinese Revolution was the Preparatory Office of the National Revolution Museum. It was founded in March 1950 and given its current name

2

Schritte von Maos Mausoleum und dem Tor zur Verbotenen Stadt, wurde das von mächtigen Säulen geprägte Ursprungsgebäude des Nationalmuseums 1959 in großer Eile errichtet. Als eines der Shi A Jianzhu oder „Zehn größten Bauwerke" sollte es den zehnten Jahrestag der Volksrepublik würdigen. In nur zehn Monaten wurde der Bau vollendet, nach den im Stil des sowjetischen Klassizismus entworfenen Plänen der Tsinghua Universität und des Beijing Architectural Design Institute (BIAD), unter der architektonischen Federführung von Zhang Kaiji. Das Gebäude beherbergte die meiste Zeit über nicht ein, sondern zwei Museen. Das erste war der Geschichte Chinas gewidmet, das andere der chinesischen Revolution. Der Vorgänger des ersten war das Vorbereitende Büro des nationalen Geschichtsmuseums „Preparatory Office of the National History Museum", welches im Sommer 1912 entstand. Es war das erste Museum einer chinesischen Regierung überhaupt. Zunächst war es ab 1912 im Imperial College untergebracht und wurde später in die Verbotene Stadt verlagert. Aus Anlass der Gründung der Volksrepublik benannte man das Museum 1949 in Nationales Geschichtsmuseum Peking um. 1959 wurde es abermals umbenannt in Nationales Museum chinesischer Geschichte. Der Vorgänger des chinesischen Revolutionsmuseums war das „Vorbereitende Büro des Nationalen Revolutionsmuseums". Es wurde 1952 gegründet und erhielt seinen heutigen Namen zehn Jahre danach. Im August 1959 war der 313 Meter lange Neubau an der Ostseite des Tiananmen-Platzes fertiggestellt und am 1. Oktober desselben Jahres eröffneten beide Museen. In den folgenden Jahrzehnten gab es immer wieder Phasen, in denen das Gebäude geschlossen war; ab 2001 schließlich wurden die Ausstellungen nicht mehr als zeitgemäß betrachtet. Bevor man beide Institutionen für die Generalsanierung 2003 schloss, vereinigte man sie in einem Museum, dem Chinesischen Nationalmuseum'[2].

Im Laufe der Jahre führten die Besucherströme von Studenten oder offiziellen Delegationen zu Verschleißerscheinungen. Den Sammlungen, darunter hunderte von bedeutenden archäologischen Funden aus ganz China, konnten die veralteten Galerien überdies kaum mehr gerecht werden. Angesichts der Olympischen Spiele in Peking im Jahr 2008 sah die Regierung die Zeit für eine grundlegende Veränderung gekommen. 2004 begann die Rekonstruktion als Teil des elften Fünf-Jahres-Plans und fand unter der genauen Begutachtung des Zentralkomitees der Kommunistischen Partei und einiger Schlüsselministerien statt. Die Entscheidung der Offiziellen, in dem erweiterten Bau nicht nur chinesische Objekte und Kunstwerke auszustellen, sondern auch Raum für Wanderausstellungen aus der ganzen Welt zu schaffen, signalisierte auch eine sich verändernde Haltung. Außerdem sollte das Museum zu einem Beispiel neuester Forschungs- und Ausstellungstechnologien werden.

Ferner galt es, eine alte architektonische Unausgewogenheit zu beheben: Obwohl das ursprüngliche Museum architektonisch genauso beeindruckend wie die benachbarten Regierungsbauten war, konnte es 1959 aus Kostengründen nicht im selben Größenmaßstab wie die gigantische Große Halle des Volkes auf der anderen Seite des Tiananmen-Platzes errichtet werden. Der siebenjährige Umbau sollte das Museum in seiner Größe nun verdreifachen. Als es am 1. März 2011 eröffnete, wurde es als das größte Museum der Welt gefeiert.

Auf die Größe kommt es sehr wohl an – daraus machten die chinesischen Amtsträger keinen Hehl. Es ging um ein Symbol des nationalen Stolzes. Mitarbeiter an dem Projekt aus westlichen Ländern wurden nachdrücklich von ihren chinesischen Kollegen zu den genauen Maßen führender Museen der Welt befragt. Allerdings vermittelt das Nationalmuseum eine subtilere Botschaft, als es seine herkulischen Dimensionen vermuten lassen. Sowohl der Prozess als auch das Ergebnis des Projekts bezeugen die Kraft der Architektur, als Form des kulturellen Austauschs zu fungieren.

› Als 1999 der britische Architekt David Chipperfield mit dem Umbau des Neuen Museums auf der Berliner Museumsinsel beauftragt wurde, sprach das Bände über das deutsche Verhältnis zur kollektiven Erinnerung und nationalen Verantwortung. So deutete auch die Wahl eines deutschen Architekturbüros für den Umbau des Nationalmuseums darauf hin, dass China ganz neu über sich selbst nachdachte. Indem eine derart sensible Aufgabe ausländischen Architekten zugedacht wurde, bekundeten die chinesischen Behörden außerdem ein großes Interesse an westlicher Expertise. (Hier sei angemerkt, dass die erste internationale Ausstellung im neu eröffneten Museum der europäischen Aufklärung gewidmet war und von einem Konsortium deutscher Museen organisiert wurde.[3]) Die deutschen Architekten gaben sich ihrerseits die größte Mühe, in ihrer Vision für

ten years later. August of 1959 saw the completion of the 313-meter-long building on the east side of Tiananmen Square, and on October 1 of that year, the two museums opened to the public. The ensuing decades were punctuated by periods when the building was closed; by 2001, the museum displays were no longer deemed reflective of China's changing identity. Prior to closing down for renovations, in 2003, the two entities were merged to form a new unified institution, the National Museum of China.[2]

Having been host to a stream of visiting students and official delegations over the years, the building was showing signs of age. The museum collections, including hundreds of architectural finds from excavations around China, were not served well in the outdated galleries. With the 2008 Olympics approaching, the leadership decided that the building was ready for a makeover. Commencing in 2004, the reconstruction project was included in the Eleventh Five-Year Plan, and it proceeded under close supervision from the CPC Central Committee and several key ministries. In a sign of evolving attitudes, the officials decided to make room in the expanded museum not only for Chinese objects and artworks, but also for traveling exhibitions from around the world. They were no less intent on making the museum a standard-bearer for advanced research and exhibition technologies.

There was a lingering architectural imbalance to remedy as well. Though every bit as imposing as the neighboring government institutions, the original museum could not be completed on a scale symmetrical with the colossal Great Hall of the People, across Tiananmen Square, owing to a shortage of funds back in 1959. The seven-year reconstruction would triple the museum in size. By the arrival of the March 1, 2011, reopening, the renovated building was heralded as the world's largest.

Clearly, for the Chinese authorities, size did matter. It was a token of national pride. Western officials involved in the project fielded urgent inquiries from their Chinese counterparts about the precise dimensions of some of the world's leading museums. Yet the National Museum building conveys a more nuanced message than its Herculean dimensions suggest. Both the process and the outcome of the project testify to the power of architecture to function as a form of cultural exchange.

› Just as the choice of the British architect David Chipperfield for the reconstruction of the Neues Museum, on Berlin's Museum Island, spoke volumes about German attitudes concerning collective memory and responsibility, so too did the choice of a German architectural firm for the National Museum suggest that China was thinking of itself in new ways. In handing over such a sensitive remit to architects from abroad, the Chinese authorities were admitting to a hunger for Western expertise. (It bears noting that the museum's first international exhibition was organized by a consortium of German museums and devoted to the European Enlightenment.[3])

For their part, the German architects went to great lengths to intertwine local and global influences in their vision for the National Museum. Their approach pays respect to both aesthetic sensibilities, without tipping too far in either direction. The result is a kind of giant cultural handshake set in stone, glass, and bronze.

3

das Nationalmuseum lokale und globale Einflüsse miteinander zu verflechten. Ihr Ansatz brachte den verschiedenen ästhetischen Welten großen Respekt entgegen, ohne eine von beiden zu bevorzugen. Das Resultat ist eine Art gigantischer kultureller Handschlag aus Stein, Glas und Bronze.

4
Zehn renommierte Architekturbüros, unter ihnen Rem Koolhaas und Herzog & de Meuron, waren zu dem Architekturwettbewerb eingeladen worden. Laut der Bauaufgabe sollte der Umbau „der dynamischen Entwicklung Chinas und den steigenden kulturellen Ansprüchen des Volkes entsprechen". Aus bautechnischer Sicht verlangte das Anforderungsprofil die Wiederherstellung der ursprünglichen Struktur einschließlich der Überdachung seiner zwei Innenhöfe, dem Nord- und Südhof – der sogenannte „Erhalt-der-drei-Fassaden"-Plan. Die Architekten von Gerkan, Marg und Partner (gmp) zusammen mit CABR China Academy of Building Research gewannen den Wettbewerb und schlugen dabei zwei weitere final gesetzte Konkurrenten aus dem Rennen: Norman Foster (zusammen mit BIAD, die 1959 für die Planung verantwortlich gewesen waren) und Kohn Pederson Fox (zusammen mit ECADI East China Architectural Design & Research Institute).

Obwohl die in Hamburg ansässigen Architekten damals in Museumskreisen weniger bekannt waren als manch anderer Wettbewerber, waren sie in Deutschland für einige der größten Infrastrukturprojekte verantwortlich, in Berlin zum Beispiel für den alten und neuen Flughafen sowie den neuen Hauptbahnhof, ein Milliardenprojekt. Seit 1999 in China vertreten, unterhält gmp Niederlassungen in Peking, Shanghai und Shenzhen. Das erste Projekt in China war die Deutsche Schule in Peking. Über die Jahre entwarfen gmp Sportstadien, Bahnhöfe und Bürohochhäuser in ganz China, aber auch eine christliche Kirche, ein Schwimmzentrum und Opernhäuser für Chongqing, Qingdao und Tianjin – und den Masterplan für Lingang, eine Stadtneugründung für 800.000 Einwohner, unter anderem mit dem Entwurf eines Maritim-Museums in Form eines stilisierten Segelschiffs.

Der offizielle Startschuss für den Umbau erfolgte im März 2007. Unter der Leitung von Meinhard von Gerkan und Stephan Schütz zusammen mit Stephan Rewolle ließ sich das gmp-Team von den historischen Bauten in der direkten Nachbarschaft inspirieren. Zum Beispiel von den mit Terrakotta-Ziegeln gedeckten Dächern der Verbotenen Stadt, die vom Museum aus gut sichtbar sind. Auch die Dimension und die bewegte Geschichte des Tiananmen-Platzes[5] waren große Einflüsse. Die vordringlichste Aufgabe der Architekten war es, einen plausiblen Zusammenhang zwischen der noch vorhandenen Struktur des Altbaus und den neu entworfenen Gebäudeteilen herzustellen. Ihr Ziel war es, die klassische Architektur zu betonen und gleichzeitig in ihrem Inneren eine durch und durch moderne Institution zu installieren.

4
v.l.n.r.
Wen Jiabao, ehem. Ministerpräsident der Volksrepublik China – **Stephan Schütz**, Partner gmp – **Gerhard Schröder** ehem. Bundeskanzler der Bundesrepublik Deutschland – **Meinhard von Gerkan**, Gründungsparter gmp

f.l.t.r.
Wen Jiabao, former Prime Minister of the Peoples Republic of China – **Stephan Schütz**, Partner gmp – **Gerhard Schröder** , former Chancelor of the Federal Republic of Germany – **Meinhard von Gerkan**, Founding partner gmp

5

Ten renowned architects, including Rem Koolhaas and Herzog & de Meuron, were invited to submit proposals. The refurbished institution, the guidelines stated, "should correspond with the dynamic development of China and the increasing cultural demand of the people." From a technical standpoint, the brief called for rebuilding the original structure and roofing over its two courtyards, the North and South Yards — the so-called Retaining Three Façades scheme. The architects von Gerkan, Marg und Partner (gmp) – CABR China Academy of Building Research team won the competition, beating two finalists: Norman Foster (allied with BIAD, which had also been responsible for the 1959 plans) and Kohn Pederson Fox (allied with ECADI East China Architectural Design & Research Institute).

Though less well known in museum circles than some of the other competing teams, the Hamburg-based gmp had been responsible for several of Germany's largest infrastructure projects, including Berlin's old and new airports and its billion-dollar central rail station. Present in China since 1999, the firm maintains offices in Beijing, Shanghai, and Shenzhen; its first project there was a school for the German embassy. Over the years, it has designed sports stadia, transport hubs, and office towers around China, and its winning commissions have included a Christian church; an aquatic center in Shanghai; theaters for Chongqing, Qingdao, and Tianjin; and a master plan for Lingang, a city of 800,00, complete with a maritime museum in the form of a sail ship.

The renovation was officially launched in March of 2007. The gmp team, headed by Meinhard von Gerkan and Stephan Schütz, together with Stephan Rewolle, took inspiration from the historic sites in the vicinity. The terra-cotta roofs of the Forbidden City are clearly visible from the museum. The scale and historic resonance of Tiananmen Square[5] were powerful influences. The task for the architects, above all, was to create a plausible cohesion between the remaining portions of the old structure and the newly built sections. They aimed to highlight the classic architecture while installing a thoroughly modern institution inside its envelope.

Above all, the gmp team wanted to make the museum more accessible. Today's architects often seek to open up and humanize older museum buildings, which typically command respect, but not so much affection from their audiences. In the submitted competition plans, the slender columns and breezy arcades of the 1959 structure formed a transition into a dramatically enlarged entry hall. The architects imagined this space as nothing less than an extension of Tiananmen Square.[6] The central core of Beijing offers scant refuge from the capital's bustle and inclement weather. What if the inside of the museum could function as a weather-protected public forum?

6

gmp wollte vor allem die Zugänglichkeit des Museums verbessern. Heutige Architekten sind oft darum bemüht, alte Museumsgebäude zu öffnen und zu „vermenschlichen", weil diese in der Regel zwar den Respekt, nicht aber die Sympathie des Publikums gewinnen. Die Wettbewerbspläne zeigten also, wie die schlanken Säulen und offenen Arkaden von 1959 in eine dramatisch vergrößerte Eingangshalle führten. In der Vorstellung der Architekten sollte dieser Raum nicht weniger als eine Erweiterung des Tiananmen-Platzes sein‘[6]. Das Zentrum von Peking bietet wenig Rückzugsmöglichkeiten vor dem geschäftigen Treiben der Hauptstadt oder schlechtem Wetter. Wie aber, wenn das Museumsinnere als wettergeschütztes öffentliches Forum funktionieren würde…?

Die Idee, ein Museum in eine Bühne öffentlicher Aktivität zu verwandeln, entsprach ganz dem neuen Museumsdenken. Der Louvre in Paris, das Britische Museum in London bis hin zum Metropolitan Museum of Art in New York – all diese Institutionen beanspruchen eine zunehmend volksnahe Rolle als einer der letzten städtischen Orte im klassischen Sinn der „Gemeinde". Sie sind nicht länger nur Refugium für Experten und Eliten – das

7

Museum des 21. Jahrhunderts möchte zum öffentlichen Platz werden, sicher, offen für alle; zu einem Ort, an dem Menschen jeglichen Hintergrunds jenseits von Shopping, Entertainment oder Religion zusammenkommen können. Die großzügigen Plazas, Innenhöfe, Dachterrassen und Gärten dieser Institutionen sprechen für das Vorhaben, das Museum zu einem Mikrokosmos der Metropole zu machen.

Dem Vorschlag der Architekten zufolge hätte man für die riesige Eingangshalle[7] die Mehrzahl der Ausstellungs- und Funktionsflächen in das Basement, die Obergeschosse sowie die Seitenflügel verlagern müssen. Der Kern des Konzepts sah vor, die Dauerausstellungen in dem obersten Geschoss unterzubringen. Demgemäß setzte das erste gmp-Entwurfskonzept auf eine dramatische architektonische Maßnahme: ein gewaltiges Bronzedach[8], das über den Innenhöfen des Museums „schweben" und unter seinen enormen „Flügeln" diverse auf die Stadt herabblickende Ausstellungsbereiche[9] versammeln sollte. Die Galerien der Dauerausstellung hätten somit eine direkte Blickbeziehung zu den bekanntesten Sehenswürdigkeiten Pekings gehabt, zum Beispiel zum Tor des Himmlischen Friedens und der Verbotenen Stadt. Das schwebende Dach wäre ein starkes Zeichen und ein Publikumsmagnet geworden. Allerdings stellte es eine Abkehr von der Bestandsarchitektur dar. So hätte es einen deutlichen Bruch zu der Fassadenkolonnade gegeben – dem wichtigsten Bestandteil des originalen Bauwerks von 1959. Dieser Eingriff erwies sich als zu radikal für den chinesischen Bauherrn.

Mehrere Überarbeitungen des Entwurfs folgten; es kam zu einer fundamentalen Neuauslegung der Grundrisse. Die Gespräche dazu fanden im Vorfeld der Olympischen Spiele statt, zu einer Zeit, als die Stimmung in den lokalen Architektenkreisen sich gegen imageträchtige westliche Bauprojekte zu wenden begann. Dem Eindruck, die chinesische Hauptstadt verwandle sich in ein Labor für experimentelle internationale Architektur, begegnete man mit immer mehr Skepsis. Hochrangige Vertreter aus der Politik nahmen Anstoß an den Entwürfen. Der Museumsdirektor Lu Zhangshen, selbst ein ausgebildeter Architekt, stoppte das Projekt und beauftragte die deutschen Architekten erneut mit der Überarbeitung. Nach dem Beschluss mehrerer Expertenkommissionen mussten die Architekten die Ausstellungsflächen in den unteren Geschossen vergrößern und eine engere Verzahnung der alten mit den neuen Gebäudeteilen herstellen.

8

The idea of making the museum a staging ground for public activities dovetailed with recent thinking about museums. From the Louvre in Paris to the British Museum in London to New York's Metropolitan Museum of Art, collecting institutions are claiming a more populist role as our last truly civic environments. No longer just a refuge for experts and the elite, the twenty-first-century museum aspires to be a public square, safe and open to all — a place where people of all backgrounds can commune free from the interferences of shopping, entertainment, and worship. The expansive plazas, courtyards, roofs, and gardens in these institutions testify to the ambition to turn the museum into a microcosm of the metropolis.

As proposed by the architects, the gargantuan entry hall[7] would have required shifting the bulk of the exhibition space and various support functions to the upper levels, basement, and side wings of the building. The linchpin of this configuration would have been the repositioning of the permanent-collection galleries to the top floor. Correspondingly, the first gmp proposal was organized around a dramatic architectural gesture: an enormous bronze roof[8] that would hover over the courtyards, its vast span encompassing a series of exhibition spaces[9] overlooking the city below. The collection would thus have been presented in direct view of Beijing's key historic sites, including the Gate of Heavenly Peace and the Forbidden City. The floating roof would have been a powerful signature and a major audience draw for the museum. But it represented a departure from the existing architecture, including a marked disconnect between the existing façade colonnade — the last element from the 1959 building that would remain intact after the reconstruction — and the newly built interior volumes. The intervention proved too radical for the Chinese clients.

Several revisions ensued, leading to a fundamental reassessment of the plan. The discussions took place during the lead-up to the Olympics, when opinion in Beijing architectural circles began to turn against high-profile Western building projects. Skepticism was on the rise about the Chinese capital becoming a laboratory for experimental international architecture. Senior officials took issue with the plans, and the museum's director, Lu Zhangshen, himself a trained architect, halted the project and sent the architects back to the drawing board. After the convening of several expert panels, the director presented the architects with a need for more exhibition space on the lower floors and a demand for tighter integration of the old and new portions of the building.

It was a difficult moment. The central element of the competition design had to be scaled back, a full year into project development and under mounting time pressure. The museum leaders and the architects deliberated the matter with the local design partner, CABR. The German team concluded that the new guidelines amounted to more than a revision. They restarted the planning process with an entirely new set of target parameters. In the revised and final plans, the roof ended up housing a large multifunction hall (Jade Hall), a suite of reception rooms, and a restaurant. The historic exhibits were moved to lower gallery floors. The public space on the ground level was reduced by more than half of its originally proposed dimensions. The completion date was pushed back past the Olympics. All this, too, is part of the back-and-forth of cultural exchange. The National Museum we see today bears the imprint not only of cultural dialogue, but also of cultural compromise.

9

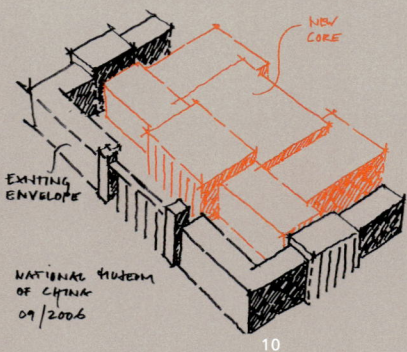

Es war ein schwieriger Moment: Das zentrale Element des Wettbewerbsentwurfs musste, nachdem man schon ein Jahr daran gearbeitet hatte und unter steigendem Zeitdruck stand, zurückgenommen werden. Die Museumsleitung und die Architekten koordinierten dies mit dem architektonischen Partnerbüro CABR vor Ort. gmp kam schließlich zu dem Ergebnis, dass die neuen Vorgaben mehr als eine Revision verlangten. Die Planung wurde unter neuen Entwurfsparametern wieder aufgenommen. In dem überarbeiteten und nun endgültigen Entwurf siedelte man im Dach einen großen Multifunktionssaal (Jade Hall), eine Reihe von Empfangsräumen und ein Restaurant an. Die historischen Exponate wurden in darunter liegende Galerieetagen verlagert, während die öffentliche Fläche im Erdgeschoss um mehr als die Hälfte der ursprünglichen Dimension verkleinert wurde. Außerdem verschob man den Fertigstellungstermin auf einen Zeitpunkt nach den Olympischen Spielen. Doch auch solche Dinge gehören zu dem Hin und Her eines kulturellen Austauschs. Das Nationalmuseum, so wie wir es heute sehen, ist nicht nur durch kulturellen Dialog, sondern auch durch kulturellen Kompromiss geprägt.

› Mit einer Bruttogeschossfläche von ungefähr 197.000 Quadratmetern und einer Kapazität von mindestens 50.000 Besuchern lässt das 380 Millionen Dollar teure Nationalmuseum keinen Zweifel an Chinas kräftigen Ambitionen. Seine 48 Ausstellungsgalerien; sein Theater mit 712 und sein Kino mit 264 Sitzen; das hochmoderne digitale Sendestudio; die Forschungsbibliothek und die Restaurierungswerkstätten; die Hotelzimmer für Künstler und Wissenschaftler; die VIP-Empfangsräume, die Festsäle und das Dachterrassenrestaurant – das alles wurde auch gebaut, um zu beeindrucken.

Vom Tiananmen-Platz aus gesehen, präsentiert sich das Museum als eine Komposition aus drei ungefähr gleich großen Baukörpern. Die beiden etwas niedrigeren nördlichen und südlichen Flanken vereinen sich in dem aufwändig verzierten Portikus. Dieser zentrale Teil ragt in den Platz hinein und wird gekrönt von der aus dem Vorgängerbau stammenden originalen Skulptur aus roten Revolutionsflaggen. Die rechteckigen Säulen des Portikus sind fast 40 Meter hoch. Dahinter befindet sich ein offener Eingangsplatz, der die historische Fassade von den neuen Museumsräumen trennt[10].

Das Museum hat nicht nur eine mehr als 300 Meter lange Front auf der Seite des Tiananmen-Platzes, sondern es erstreckt sich auch über 200 Meter entlang der mehrspurigen und vielbefahrenen Durchgangsstraße Chang An East Road[11]. Gemäß der Wettbewerbsausschreibung umschließen die restaurierten Fassaden den neuen Kern des Museums an drei Seiten. Aus der Entfernung sind die hervorgehobenen bronzefarbenen Dachkanten der einzige Hinweis auf das moderne Innere. Aus der Vogelperspektive offenbart das Museum zwei begrünte Innenhöfe, die von Rehwaldt Landschaftsarchitekten aus Dresden entworfen wurden. Für den südlichen Innenhof schuf das Büro eine abstrakte chinesische Wasserlandschaft, für den nördlichen Hof eine Gebirgslandschaft.

Das hervorstechende Merkmal des Gebäudes ist nicht mehr die Dachkonstruktion, sondern das nicht ohne Grund so genannte Grand Forum[12] – beziehungsweise das, was von dem Bestreben der Architekten übrigblieb, den Tiananmen-Platz in das Museum zu holen. Obwohl kleiner als ursprünglich geplant, ist das Forum immer noch atemberaubend. Es umfasst nahezu 9000 Quadratmeter und ist um ein Viertel größer als die Turbinenhalle der Tate Modern in London. Hier wird der Besucher

11

› With a completed floor area of approximately 197,000 square meters and room inside to comfortably host 50,000 people, the 380-million-dollar museum that emerged from the planning process leaves no doubt about China's muscular ambitions. Its forty-eight exhibition halls, its 712-seat operatic theatre and 264-seat cinema, its state-of-the-art digital broadcast studio, its research library and conservation center, its hotel accommodations for visiting artists and scientists, its VIP reception rooms — all were built to impress.

Viewed from Tiananmen Square, the structure presents itself as a composite of three roughly equal masses. The slightly lower northern and southern flanks come together in a heavily ornamented portico. This central portion protrudes into the square, capped with a sculptural riot of crimson revolutionary flags preserved from the old construction. The rectangular columns of the portico reach up almost forty meters. Behind them lies an open corridor that marks off the historic façade from the new interior mass of the building.[10]

In addition to its more than 300 meters of frontage on Tiananmen Square, the museum stretches back 200 meters on Chang An East Road,[11] a heavily trafficked multilane thoroughfare. As per the competition brief, restored façades envelop the all-new central core on three sides. From a distance, the only clues to the modern inner core are the elevated bronze-colored rooflines. An aerial view of the building reveals two planted courtyards, designed by the Dresden-based Rehwaldt Landscape Architects, which created an abstract Chinese water landscape for the South Yard and mountain landscape for the North Yard.

The building's signature is no longer the roof, but the aptly named Grand Forum[12] — or what remains of the architect's desire to bring Tiananmen Square into the museum. Though smaller than originally envisioned, it is still breathtaking. Its almost 9,000 square-meter footprint is 25 % larger than the London Tate Modern's Turbine Hall. This is the receiving hub of the museum, containing an array of visitor services such as cloakrooms, information counters, cafés, bathrooms, and bookshops.

Unfortunately, some features added since the opening do not conform to the building's overall design. Functionally speaking, the Grand Forum connects the northern and southern wings of the museum. It is a gathering point for visitors before they disperse inward through a large viewing gallery for socialist realist art, and upward, via stairs and escalators, toward the interior galleries and the educational, administrative, and hospitality spaces of the museum. Bathed in western light pouring in through a glass wall that spans the Forum's 260-meter length and 27-meter height, the staggering entry hall, even in its diminished form, is destined to be one of the iconic interiors of modern China.

Once inside the museum, the visitor cannot escape noticing the blend of Eastern and Western idioms. Although conventional white-box galleries take up much of the building, hints are everywhere to be found of Chinese styles and traditions. The German architects continue a conversation that started with the building's original plans. The original Chinese architects were clearly steeped in European aesthetics. They produced a structure that was ornamented in the traditional style, most prominently on its handsome terra-cotta-laced eaves (some pieces were remanufactured for the renovation in the same factory that had made them in 1959), yet was at once recognizably European. Similar buildings sprouted up in socialist capitals in Eastern Europe throughout the 1950s. A half-century later, the German architects began their task by imagining an archetype of a Chinese building. This would shape the forms and materials of the new structure.

12

im Museum empfangen, hier befinden sich die Informationsschalter, Cafés, Buchläden, Garderoben und Toiletten. Leider wurden seit der Eröffnung einige Dinge hinzugefügt, die nicht zu dem Gesamtkonzept des Gebäudes passen. Aus funktionaler Sicht verbindet das Grand Forum den Nord- mit dem Südflügel. Es ist ein Sammelpunkt für die Besucher, bevor sie durch die große Galerie für die Kunst des Sozialistischen Realismus gehen und dann über Treppen und Rolltreppen hinauf zu den innen gelegenen Galerien, den Vortragssälen und zu den administrativen und gastronomischen Bereichen gelangen. Die Eingangshalle, getaucht in das Licht, das von Westen her durch eine 260 Meter lange und 27 Meter hohe gläserne Fassade dringt, ist trotz ihrer verkleinerten Ausführung dazu bestimmt, eine der Innenraum-Ikonen des modernen China zu werden.

Sobald der Besucher im Inneren des Museums ist, wird ihm die Mischung aus westlichen und fernöstlichen Stilen auffallen. Obwohl die meisten Ausstellungshallen im konventionellen „white box"-Stil gehalten sind, befinden sich überall Hinweise auf chinesische Attribute und Traditionen. Hier führen die deutschen Architekten einen Dialog fort, der mit den Originalplänen des Gebäudes begann: Schon die Erbauer des ursprünglichen Museums waren eindeutig von einer europäischen Ästhetik beeinflusst. Sie schufen ein Bauwerk, das im Stil der traditionellen Ornamentik geschmückt war – sehr augenscheinlich war dies an der Dachtraufe zu erkennen, die mit Terrakotta verkleidet war – und dennoch erkennbar europäisch wirkte (einige Bauteile wurden während der Sanierung in derselben Fabrik wie 1959 wieder neu hergestellt). Stilistisch ähnlich geartete Bauten entstanden während der 1950er Jahre auch in anderen sozialistischen Hauptstädten Osteuropas. Wiederum ein halbes Jahrhundert später nahmen die deutschen Architekten ihre Arbeit auf, indem sie sich den Archetyp eines chinesischen Gebäudes vorstellten – eine Vorstellung, die Form und Material der neuen Struktur prägen sollte.

Die wesentlichen Komponenten traditioneller chinesischer Architektur sind im gmp-Entwurf vorhanden: Das Bauwerk ruht auf einem Fundament aus Granit, der aus der Region stammt. Klassische Holzkonstruktionen werden durch großflächige Kirschholzpaneele in der Verkleidung der inneren Wände des Grand Forums aufgenommen. Die Wandpaneele der Festhalle im obersten Geschoss, der Eingangsebene und des Theaters sind mit eigens hergestelltem, schallschluckendem Gewebe in Purpur verkleidet – die historische Farbe Chinas. Die VIP-Räume im Erdgeschoss wurden von Frau Professor Zhang von der Central Academy of Fine Arts in Peking entworfen, die schon an Maos Mausoleum und den Empfangsräumen der Großen Halle des Volkes gearbeitet hatte. Die gestaffelten weißen Metallträger des neuen Museumsdachs sind ein zartes Echo der traditionellen Dachkonstruktion in der unmittelbaren Umgebung. Die großen bronzenen Eingangstüren[13] wurden vom traditionellen chinesischen Metallhandwerk inspiriert und in einer zurückhaltenden westlichen Interpretation wiedergegeben. Sie filtern durch ihre klöppelspitzenartige Perforation Tageslicht in das Grand Forum und versehen so die kathedraleske Größe des Raums mit Wärme und Textur. Außerdem sorgen sie für einen visuellen Bezug zu einem wertvollen Bronzegefäß in der Sammlung.

Im Abwägen zwischen chinesischen und westlichen Designphilosophien musste gmp einen Drahtseilakt absolvieren. Schiere Imitation kam nicht in Frage – das hätte das Museum zu einem architektonischen Themenpark gemacht. Andererseits hätte ein allzu offener Stilkonflikt ein misstönendes postmodernes Pastiche erzeugen können. Die Herausforderung bestand darin, ein fein austariertes Geben-und-Nehmen zwischen westlicher und fernöstlicher Tradition zu orchestrieren.

Die Architekten gingen mit großer Disziplin hinsichtlich der Materialwahl und unter Vermeidung übertrieben direkter Bezüge vor. So sind die Dächer des Museums zwar eindeutig von der Verbotenen Stadt beeinflusst, aber statt traditioneller Dachschindeln aus Keramik sind sie, zugunsten einer puristischeren und zeitgemäßeren Anmutung, mit koloriertem Metall gedeckt. Die Zahl der verwendeten Materialien wurde bewusst auf drei begrenzt – Granit, Kirschholz, Bronzelegierung – und folgt so dem modernistischen Streben nach Einheit und Beständigkeit im gesamten Gebäude. gmp musste während der Planung und Ausführung entschlossen für diese Selbstbeschränkung auf Seiten des Bauherrns streiten, denn sie läuft dem chinesischen Geschmack, Materialien zu mischen und Räume mit den verschiedensten Dekorationen zu verzieren, völlig zuwider.

The essential components of traditional Chinese architecture are in place: The structure rests on a stone base made of locally sourced granite. Classic wood construction is indicated with extensive cherry-wood paneling on interior walls in the Grand Forum. The panels of the ceremonial hall on the top floor as well as on the entrance level and in the theater are clad in a custom-made sound-absorbing fabric in a shade of crimson — China's historic color. (The VIP rooms on the ground floor were designed by professor Zhang from China Central Academy of Fine Art who had once worked for the Mao mausoleum and on reception rooms in the People's Hall.) The staggered white metal beams of the new roofs faintly echo the traditional rooflines in the immediate vicinity. The large bronze entrance gates[13] on the ground floor are inspired by traditional Chinese metalwork, reimagined here in a pared-down Western aesthetic. They filter daylight into the Grand Forum through lacelike perforations that add texture and warmth to the cathedral-like immensity of space. They also form a visual link to a bronze vessel in the museum's collection.

The gmp architects had to walk a fine line when it came to finding a balance between Chinese and Western design philosophies. Blind imitation would fall flat, making the museum an exercise in theme architecture. (Ersatz copies, in any case, had to be avoided in deference to museum norms forbidding the use of artificial objects.) On the other hand, a too overt clash of styles might have created a jarring postmodernist pastiche. The challenge was to orchestrate a subtle give-and-take between two cultural traditions.

The architects imposed discipline on the choice of materials and avoided overly direct references. The roofs, for example, are clearly inspired by the Forbidden City, but instead of traditional ceramic tiles they are finished with colored metal for a cleaner, more contemporary look. Reducing the number of recurring materials to three — granite stone, cherry wood, bronze alloy — followed a modernist impulse to achieve unity and consistency throughout the building. The German architects had to press their case for self-restraint during the design process. It runs counter to the Chinese taste for mixing materials and embellishing rooms with all manner of decorations.

13

The allusions to Chinese building methods do not end with the building's structure and materials. Further references to the Forbidden City are to be found in the columns, balustrades,[14] and ceiling coffers[15] in the Grand Forum and other representative spaces. The experience of walking from large halls into progressively smaller and more intimate spaces echoes the structure and flow of the Forbidden City. Here and there, the building defers to ancient Feng Shui principles. Sharp corners and turns have been avoided. Indirect paths are preferred over direct ones. The upper level is not accessed through a central staircase, as would be the case in a Western museum. Instead, visitors ascend along a roundabout path, via a pair of stairs on either side of the Grand Forum. The gesture gives expression to the Feng Shui "ghost wall" ('ying bi'), a perpendicular obstruction placed directly in front of the entranceway of traditional Chinese houses, warding off intruding bad spirits.

One eye-catching reference was by all accounts unintentional: the stone staircase balustrades in the Grand Forum appear to mimic, in the abstract, the contours of the Great Wall of China. The architects insist that this particular reference was coincidental. Might the German designers have internalized the local context so deeply as to be inadvertently inspired by it? If so, this would arguably be the most genuine expression of the cultural osmosis fueling the design process.

14

Die Anspielungen auf chinesische Bauweisen erschöpfen sich nicht in Material und Struktur des Gebäudes. Weitere Hinweise auf die Verbotene Stadt finden sich in den Säulen, Balustraden[14] und den Kassettendecken[15] des Grand Forum und weiterer repräsentativer Räume. Die Besuchererfahrung, von großen Hallen in stets kleinere und intimere Räume zu gelangen, ist ein Nachhall der Struktur und des Verlaufs der Verbotenen Stadt. Hier und da verbeugt sich das Museum auch vor alten Feng-Shui-Prinzipien. Spitze Winkel und Ecken wurden vermieden. Indirekte Wegführung wird direkter vorgezogen. Die oberen Geschosse erschließen sich nicht über ein zentrales Treppenhaus, wie es in einem westlichen Museum wohl der Fall wäre. Stattdessen steigen die Besucher, wie auf einem Rundkurs, über zwei Treppen an je einer Seite des Grand Forums auf. Diese Vorgehensweise bezieht sich auf die „Geisterwand" (Ying Bi) des Feng Shui, eine Sichtblende, die direkt vor den Eingängen traditioneller chinesischer Häuser steht, um böse Geister abzuwehren.

Eine augenfällige Referenz entstand jedoch ganz und gar unabsichtlich: Die Balustraden der Steintreppe im Grand Forum ähneln in ihren Umrissen der Chinesischen Mauer. Die Architekten versichern, dass dieser besondere Bezug zufällig zustande kam. Haben die deutschen Designer den regionalen Kontext vielleicht so verinnerlicht, dass sie von ihm auch ungewollt inspiriert wurden? Wenn dem so ist, dann wäre dies der authentischste Beweis dafür, wie kulturelle Osmose den Entwurfsprozess antreiben kann.

Kultureller Austausch bedeutet nicht nur die Amalgamierung von Stilen und Traditionen, sondern auch die gegenseitige Teilhabe an Fachwissen. In Bezug auf die Ausstellungs- und Forschungstechnik war der Einfluss recht einseitig – von West nach Ost. Das war bei chinesischen Museen schon lange so gewesen. Im 19. Jahrhundert erreichte die europäische Mode der Museumsbauten auch China. Die Idee eines Nationalmuseums als Verkörperung kollektiver Identität ist natürlich eine europäische Erfindung, die auf der ganzen Welt enthusiastisch kopiert wurde. Obwohl in letzter Zeit sehr viele Museen in China entstanden sind, bleiben sie im Großen und Ganzen eine westliche Technologie – und die Entschlossenheit, mit der sich China diese Technologie aneignet, ist beeindruckend. Fürs Erste jedoch bleiben die wissenschaftlichen, kuratorischen und technischen Fähigkeiten chinesischer Museen noch hinter denen ihrer westlichen Pendants zurück.

Nach dem Willen der Behörden sollte das Nationalmuseum nach der Sanierung und dem Umbau die in operativer Hinsicht modernste Kunsteinrichtung Chinas sein. Es sollte einen neuen Standard setzen, nicht nur in seiner Größe, sondern auch in der Vervollkommnung aller operativen Aspekte – von seinen museologischen, wissenschaftlichen und pädagogischen Funktionen bis hin zu seinem gigantischen Apparat von hinter den Kulissen wirkenden haustechnischen-Systemen. Deutschland bot sich als Partner für diesen Austausch technischen Wissens an. Keinem Land verdanken die westlichen Konzepte von Kunstmuseen mehr als Deutschland, und China hatte von der infrastrukturellen Expertise der Deutschen stets eine hohe Meinung. Die professionellen Beziehungen, die zu der architektonischen Zusammenarbeit mit Deutschland führten, waren bereits älter als ein Jahrzehnt.

14

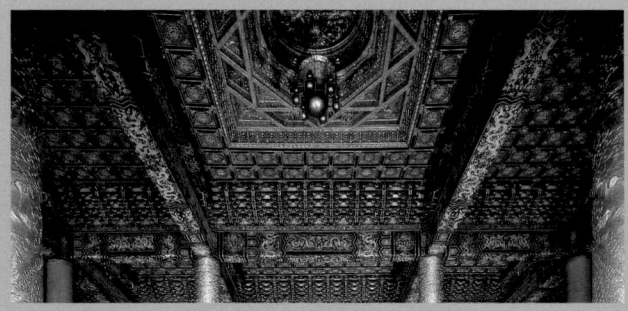

15

Cultural exchange involves not just the amalgamation of styles and traditions, but also the sharing of professional expertise. When it comes to the National Museum's exhibiting and research functions, the influences flowed mainly in one direction – from West to East. This has long been the case for Chinese museums. The European fashion of building museums was introduced to China in the nineteenth century. The notion of the national museum as an embodiment of collective identity is, of course, a European invention that has been enthusiastically copied worldwide. Although museums have proliferated in China of late, they remain, by and large, a Western technology – a technology that China is adopting with impressive resolve. For now, however, the scholarly, curatorial, and technical capabilities of Chinese museums still lag behind those of their Western counterparts.

For the refurbished National Museum, the authorities set out to create the most operationally advanced art institution in China. The museum would need to set a new standard not just with its size, but through the sophistication of its operations – from its museological, research, and educational functions to the vast array of behind-the-scenes building systems. Germany was a natural partner for this exchange of technical know-how. Western notions of art museums owe as much to Germany as to any nation, and Chinese opinion has long held German infrastructural expertise in high regard. The professional relationships that led to the architectural collaboration with Germany stretched back more than a decade. Over the course of the project, the German architects weighed in on countless aspects of the museum, going well beyond their core design mandate. They proposed up-to-date lighting and acoustic solutions as well as ventilation and climate systems in the exhibition halls. They watched over the execution of every construction detail. In a country where museums often are conceived with scant advance thinking about their programming, the mission of the new National Museum evolved through sustained interaction with the Western architects. It is hard to say where such influences begin or end. Yet it is not too far-fetched to suggest that the broadening of the museum's global mandate – resulting in dedicated galleries for exhibits from Europe, Asia, Africa, and America – may have owed something to the prolonged intercultural collaboration that propelled the institution to its final form.

› A remarkable aspect of China's epic investments into cultural facilities has been the degree to which they are driven by an impulse to communicate with the world. The hundreds of museums now being built around the country are intended to project China's prestige abroad and to absorb cultural influences that China's citizens will need to operate in a global society in which they are claiming a larger role. China's cultural output now ranks with those of the largest industrialized nations, and is growing rapidly. Much of the new cultural activity is designed with the rest of the world in mind. More than eighty billion dollars were spent on huge soft-power initiatives, such as the 2008 Olympics and the 2010 World Expo. The Chinese art market has increased its market share more than fourfold since 1996, becoming the second largest after the United States. Hundreds of Confucius Institutes and thousands of arts administrators labor each day to nurture engagement between China and other nations.

Im Laufe des Projekts brachten sich die deutschen Architekten in zahllose Fragen bezüglich des Museums ein und gingen dabei weit über ihr eigentliches architektonisches Mandat hinaus. Sie schlugen modernste Beleuchtungs- und Beschallungslösungen vor, genauso wie Belüftungs- und Klimasysteme in den Ausstellungsräumen. Sie überwachten jedes Detail der Bauausführung. In einem Land, in dem Museen oft ohne langfristiges Programmdenken geplant werden, entwickelte sich die Mission des neuen Nationalmuseums durch die nachhaltige Interaktion mit den Architekten aus dem Westen. Schwer zu sagen, wo solche Einflussnahme beginnt oder endet. Dennoch geht es nicht zu weit zu behaupten, dass die globale Ausrichtung des Museums – in Form von Ausstellungsgalerien für Europa, Asien, Afrika und Amerika – auch der langen interkulturellen Zusammenarbeit geschuldet ist.

› An den epischen Ausmaßen, mit denen China in seine kulturellen Einrichtungen investiert, ist ein Aspekt besonders bemerkenswert: wieviel sie mit dem Bedürfnis nach Kommunikation mit der Welt zu tun haben. Die Hundertschaften von Museen, die derzeit im ganzen Land gebaut werden, sollen Chinas Prestige im Ausland fördern und zugleich jene kulturellen Einflüsse absorbieren, die seine Bürger brauchen, um sich in der globalen Gesellschaft, in der sie eine größere Rolle beanspruchen, behaupten zu können. Chinas kulturelle Produktion ist heute vergleichbar mit der der größten Industrienationen — und sie wächst rasant. Viel von dieser neuen kulturellen Aktivität wird mit dem Rest der Welt im Hinterkopf angegangen. Mehr als 80 Milliarden Dollar wurden in gewaltige „soft power"-Initiativen gesteckt, wie zum Beispiel die Olympischen Spiele von 2008 oder die World Expo 2010. Der chinesische Kunstmarkt hat seinen Marktanteil seit 1996 mehr als vervierfacht und ist inzwischen der zweitgrößte hinter dem der USA. Hunderte von Konfuzius-Instituten und Tausende von Kunst- und Kulturmanagern bzw. Kunsthändlern arbeiten täglich am kulturellen Austausch von China mit anderen Nationen.

Die Maßgabe, 100 Museen im Jahr zu errichten – wahrscheinlich der größte Museumsbauboom, den die Welt jemals sehen wird – steht natürlich im Zusammenhang mit der Eröffnung des Chinesischen Nationalmuseums. Allerdings sollte man den Erfolg der chinesischen Investitionen in Museen nicht nur in Zahlen ausdrücken, sondern vor allem in der Art und Weise, wie man durch diese, mit und von diesen neuen Einrichtungen lernt; in den subtilen Wirkungen, die sie auf individuelle Identitäten und kollektive Bindungen ausüben werden. Das gilt auch für das Chinesische Nationalmuseum. Seine rekordverdächtige Größe, 1,2 Millionen Ausstellungsstücke, acht Millionen Besucher im Jahr sind ohne Zweifel überwältigend. Dennoch wird das wahre Maß seiner Errungenschaften darin bestehen, dass es Standards für andere Museen in China zu setzen vermag und, was noch wichtiger ist, inwieweit es den chinesischen Bürgern dabei helfen kann, sich mehr als bisher global zu orientieren und zu informieren und sich selbst mehr als bisher zu reflektieren. Im Falle von Museen gehen solche Ansprüche weit über Architektur hinaus. Aber dort nehmen sie ihren Anfang.

In den kommenden Jahren werden die Museen Chinas ihren Stand in der globalen Bedeutung und in Chinas eigener kultureller Ökologie zu festigen trachten. Ihr Personal und ihre Ausstellungen werden mit der Zeit besser werden, weil sie von einer besseren Ausbildung, zunehmender Erfahrung und einer aufstrebenden Wirtschaft profitieren werden. Wenn das wichtigste Museum in China eine Lektion für all die vielen Institutionen bereithält, die überall im Land aus dem Boden schießen, dann ist es diese: Kultur kann nicht alleine gedeihen. Kultur lebt von Dialog und Gegenseitigkeit. Sie verlangt die Kunst des Zuhörens. Kultur beruht auf einer ständigen Suche nach Symmetrie und Harmonie – zwischen der Vergangenheit und der Gegenwart, innen und außen, uns und den anderen. Das neue Gebäude des Chinesischen Nationalmuseums zeigt uns, dass diese Suche, auch wenn deren letztes Ziel selten klar ist, am besten im Zusammenspiel mit den Menschen aufgenommen wird, die keine Angst davor haben, ihre Visionen und Talente zu teilen.

New York, Dezember 2012

Dieser Essay ist die veränderte und beträchtlich erweiterte Version eines Artikels des Autors über das chinesische Nationalmuseum in „The Art Newspaper", April 2011.

The policy of erecting one hundred museums a year – most likely the largest museum-construction spree the world will ever witness – is part of this grand opening. Yet the success of China's museum investments should not be measured only in numbers. The most relevant outcome will be the quality of the learning experience that the new institutions provide, the subtle effects they are destined to have on individual identities and collective bonds. The same is true of the National Museum of China. Its vital statistics – its record-size building, its 1.2 million objects, its eight million visitors – are awesome beyond dispute. The true measure of the museum's achievement, nonetheless, will be whether it can set progressive norms for other museums around China, and more important, whether it can help nurture a more globally informed and self-aware Chinese citizenry. For museums, such aspirations admittedly go well beyond architecture. But they begin with it.

In the years to come, Chinese museums will continue to seek their footing in terms of global relevance and within China's own cultural ecology. Their staffs and exhibitions should improve with time, benefitting from better training, more experience, and an ascendant economy. If the most important museum in China has a lesson for the many new institutions now sprouting up around the country, it is that culture cannot prosper alone. It feeds on dialogue and reciprocity. It demands listening skills. Culture consists of a perpetual search for symmetry and harmony – between past and present, inside and outside, us and them. The National Museum of China's building tells us that this search, although its ultimate destination is seldom clear, is best undertaken in alliance with people who are not afraid to share their visions and talents.

New York, December 2012

This essay was adapted and significantly expanded from an article by the author about the National Museum of China in "The Art Newspaper", April 2011.

Eine deutsch-chinesische Zusammenarbeit

Ein Interview mit Stephan Schütz [gmp] und Ma Lidong [CABR]
moderiert von Zhou Rong

Zhou Rong Ich freue mich über die Gelegenheit, ausführlich mit Stephan Schütz und Ma Lidong sprechen zu können. Seit 1998, der Entstehung des ersten gmp-Büros in China, haben von Gerkan, Marg und Partner über 150 Projekte in China realisiert. Dazu zählen sehr wichtige öffentliche Projekte, wie zum Beispiel das Chinesische Nationalmuseum. Zwar sind in den vergangenen zehn Jahren zahlreiche ausländische Büros neu in den chinesischen Architekturmarkt gekommen, aber viele ihrer Projekte passen einfach nicht zu dem Ort, an dem sie gebaut wurden. Das ist bei gmp anders, und deshalb ist das Büro in China auch so erfolgreich. gmp ist ein sehr lebendiges und konkurrenzfähiges internationales Büro geworden. Stephan Schütz, gibt es so etwas wie gmp-„Geheimtipps", die diesen Erfolg erklären?

Stephan Schütz Von Geheimtipps kann man sicherlich nicht sprechen. Ich glaube, es ist die grundsätzliche Haltung zur Architektur, die seit der Gründung des Büros konsequent entwickelt wurde. Die Konsequenz dieser Haltung erkennt man bei jedem Projekt von gmp. Sie ist mit dem Begriff „Dialog" oder „Dialogisches Entwerfen" zu beschreiben. Mit Dialog ist ein Austausch über das, was gebaut werden soll, gemeint, aber natürlich auch die Auseinandersetzung mit der Kultur und dem Ort unserer Bauaufgaben. Letztendlich ist unsere Arbeit immer auch ein Dialog mit der spezifischen Aufgabe, die die Bedürfnisse des Bauherrn oder der Nutzer widerspiegelt. Nur wenn man zu diesem Dialog bereit ist, entstehen Bauwerke, die aus der Komplexität und Vielzahl von Anforderungen etwas Einzigartiges hervorbringen. Dabei spielen Erfahrungen aus dem eigenen Kulturkreis eine ebenso wichtige Rolle wie Hinzuerworbenes aus bis dato fremden Sphären.

Zhou Rong Trotz großer Unterschiede zwischen der chinesischen und der deutschen Kultur feiert gmp bei vielen öffentlichen Architekturwettbewerben in China immer wieder große Erfolge. Dabei ist die chinesische Kultur viel flexibler und variabler. Sie lässt sich viel stärker von emotionalen Faktoren beeinflussen und neigt zum Denken in Symbolen. Die deutsche Kultur hingegen geht mit der Welt viel rationaler um. Die Deutschen denken eher logisch und verantwortungsbewusst, ihre Technik ist sehr präzise. Die Frage ist: Wie schafft es gmp, trotz dieses enormen kulturellen Unterschieds die Vorstellung der Bauherren exakt zu erfassen und architektonisch widerzuspiegeln?

Stephan Schütz Wenn wir uns bewusst machen, dass die chinesische Sprache eine Bildersprache ist, wird die Frage nach Image oder Symbol in China sehr verständlich. China ist eine Nation, die sich wirtschaftlich unglaublich schnell entwickelt und die zugleich auf eine sehr lange Tradition zurückschauen kann. Die allerorten spürbare Frage ist, wie sich beides verbinden lässt.

Die Identität eines mächtigen Landes, das eine Balance zwischen Tradition und Moderne sucht, basiert im Fall von China auch auf Bildern oder Metaphern. Als Architekten nehmen wir diesen Tatbestand ernst, gleichzeitig differenzieren wir. Ich glaube, der Wunsch, etwas Symbolisches, also Bildgewaltiges zu bauen, ist berechtigt, besonders bei wichtigen öffentlichen Gebäuden. Sie stehen für die Anmutung einer Stadt, sie prägen ihr Image. Metaphorisches hat aber meiner Ansicht nach keinen Platz bei Bürogebäuden oder Wohngebäuden, die eher den städtischen Kontext repräsentieren. Das heißt, es gibt klare typologische Unterschiede bei den verschiedenen Bauaufgaben. Wäre dem nicht so, würden unsere Städte in einer architektonischen Kakophonie versinken. In China ist das leider mancherorts der Fall.

Die Verhältnisse in Deutschland sind ohnehin anders. Wir reden nicht über wachsende Städte, sondern meistenteils über schrumpfende Städte. Selbst hier in Berlin stagniert die Stadtentwicklung bezogen auf das Wachstum der Bevölkerung. Die Identität unserer Städte ist in großem Maße durch ein gewachsenes Stadtbild vorgeprägt und die Neigung, Unverwechselbarkeit durch ikonografische Bauten zu schaffen, ist, von Ausnahmen abgesehen, vergleichsweise gering ausgebildet. Summa summarum führen unterschiedliche wirtschaftliche, gesellschaftliche und politische Konditionen zu unterschiedlichen Ansprüchen an Architektur und Städtebau.

A German-Chinese Cooperation

An Interview with Stephan Schütz [gmp] and Ma Lidong [CABR]
conducted by Zhou Rong

Zhou Rong   I am very pleased about the opportunity to be able to talk in detail with Stephan Schütz and Ma Lidong. Since 1998, when the first gmp office was opened in China, von Gerkan, Marg and Partners have completed over 150 projects in China. These include very important public projects such as the Chinese National Museum. Although numerous foreign practices have entered the Chinese architecture market over the last ten years, many of their projects simply do not fit in with the place at which they were built. That is different with gmp, and that is why the practice is so successful in China. gmp has become a very lively and competitive international practice. Stephan Schütz, are there any "secret tips" that might explain this success?

Stephan Schütz   I would not say that there are secret tips. But I believe that it is our fundamental approach to architecture which has been systematically developed since the opening of gmp's office. This approach shines through every project completed by gmp. It can be described by the term "dialogue" or "dialogue in design." The term "dialogue" refers to an exchange about what is going to be built and also an interaction with the culture and the spirit of the place of our projects. Ultimately our work always involves a dialogue, with the specific objective of reflecting the needs of both building owners and users. This dialogue is needed in order to design buildings that create something unique from the complexity and multiplicity of requirements. The experience from our own cultural background plays just as important a role as those elements we have to learn from the culture of foreign spheres.

Zhou Rong   In spite of the big differences between Chinese and German culture, gmp has been successful in many public architectural competitions in China. In many ways, Chinese culture is more flexible and variable. It is influenced much more by emotional factors, and symbols are often used as an expression. By contrast, German culture has a much more rational approach to dealing with the world. Germans think rather more logically and with responsibility, their method is very precise. The question is: how does gmp manage, in spite of these enormous cultural differences, to exactly capture the client's ideas and turn them into architectural reality?

Stephan Schütz   When we remember that the Chinese language is a picture language, it is not so difficult to understand the Chinese image- or symbol-based approach. China is a nation that has developed very quickly commercially and, at the same time, can look back over a very long tradition. The question that can be sensed everywhere is: how can both be combined?

The identity of a powerful country searching for a balance between tradition and the Moderne is also based on images or metaphors. As architects, we take this fact seriously while also striking a balance. I believe that the desire to build something with a powerful symbolic context is justified, particularly when it comes to important public buildings. They are an important element in the appearance of a city, and determine its image. However, I feel that metaphoric images are misplaced in offices and apartment blocks, which are more reflective of the urban context. This means that there is a clear typological difference between different building projects. Were this not so, our cities would drown in the multiplicity of architectural symbolism and metaphor. Unfortunately, that is the case in some places in China.

In Germany the conditions are different anyway. In most cases, we are not talking about growing, but about shrinking cities. Even here in Berlin, the city's development is stagnant in terms of the population size. To a large extent, the identity of our cities is predetermined by their history, and the tendency to create uniqueness through iconographic buildings is, exceptions excluded, relatively rare. In summary, we can say that different economic, social, and political conditions lead to different objectives for architecture and urban design.

Zhou Rong   gmp hat zahlreiche Projekte in China realisiert. Welche gmp-Projekte in China halten Sie für die gelungensten oder die repräsentativsten?

Stephan Schütz   Es ist sehr schwierig, einzelne Projekte herauszugreifen, weil jedes Projekt seine spezifischen Bedingungen und seine spezifische Geschichte hat. Ich will dennoch auf ein Projekt eingehen, welches das Phänomen des dialogischen Entwerfens bestens widerspiegelt – das Chinesische Nationalmuseum in Beijing.

Wie Sie wissen, haben wir das Projekt mit einem Wettbewerbsentwurf gewonnen, der stark auf den Kontrast zwischen Altbau und Erweiterung fokussierte. Ein modernes, scheinbar über dem Altbau schwebendes Dach war als weithin sichtbares Zeichen konzipiert, das die unterschiedlichen Zeitepochen der Entstehung des Nationalmuseums im Stadtraum sichtbar machen sollte. Wir haben ein Jahr lang im Dialog mit dem damaligen Bauherrn unseren Wettbewerbsentwurf vertieft, bis es zu einem Sinneswandel auf dessen Seite kam. Der eingeschlagene Weg wurde nunmehr als unangemessen für den weiteren Fortgang des Projekts angesehen, da er die historische Bedeutung des Platzes und des existierenden Museums anscheinend nicht in ausreichendem Maße würdigte.

Im Ergebnis führte das zu einem Erweiterungsbau, der die Sprache des vorhandenen Gebäudes aufnimmt und sie in zeitgemäßer Weise abstrahiert. Elemente des Altbaus werden aufgegriffen und transformiert, sodass die bauzeitlichen Entstehungsschritte für den Besucher erfahrbar werden. Der dialogische Prozess führte uns dazu, die eigene Position komplett infrage zu stellen. Ich muss hinzufügen, dass dies ein singuläres und sicherlich extremes Beispiel in der gesamten Bürogeschichte darstellt. Es zeugt aber auch von der Einsicht, dass nicht wir als Architekten bestimmen, was und wie gebaut wird, sondern dass unsere Städte und Gebäude Zeugnis eines kollektiven Prozesses sind. Wer als Architekt mit einem individuell vorbestimmten Architekturstil, mit einer rein künstlerischen Handschrift auftritt, verschließt sich meines Erachtens dem Dialog. Ich denke, zu einer erfolgreichen Architektur gehört eine offene Haltung.

Zhou Rong   Das chinesische Designinstitut CABR (China Academy of Building Research) ist eines der wichtigsten und traditionsreichsten Architekturinstitute in China. Die Zusammenarbeit in der Planung zwischen gmp und CABR war eine große Herausforderung. Beide Büros mussten sich mit den großen Unterschieden im kulturellen, planerischen und organisatorischen Denken arrangieren. Können Sie bitte mit ein paar Beispielen erläutern, wie die beiden Büros während der Kooperation miteinander kommunizierten?

Ma Lidong   Vorab ist zu sagen, dass wir schon vor dem chinesischen Nationalmuseum bei 15 oder 16 Projekten mit gmp zusammengearbeitet haben. Um aber bei diesem Beispiel zu bleiben: Wie Stephan Schütz schon andeutete, ist der Erweiterungsbau des Museums wahrscheinlich das erfolgreichste Projekt von gmp in China. Das gilt auch für CABR. Meiner Meinung nach hat dieser Erfolg zwei Gründe. Erstens hatte gmp ein sehr klares Ziel – auch darüber hat Stephan Schütz schon gesprochen. Zweitens ist beiden Büros die Kommunikation sehr wichtig. In diesem Fall war das aber besonders kompliziert. Bei gewöhnlichen Projekten müssen sich Architekturbüro, Bauherr und Baufirma austauschen. Beim chinesischen Nationalmuseum waren aber noch zwei weitere Parteien beteiligt: nämlich ein Fachexpertenteam und das Team von der Regierung. Das Expertenteam bestand aus Wu Liangyong, Zhou Ganzhi, Zhang Jinqiu, Li Daozeng, Peng Yigang, Qi Kang, Ma Guoxin und anderen. Von der Regierung war, neben anderen Behörden, die staatliche Kommission für Entwicklung und Reform dabei. Diese beiden zusätzlichen Teams haben entscheidend mitgewirkt, und sie hatten einen großen Einfluss auf das Projekt, mehr noch als bei anderen vergleichbaren Projekten. Dass also insgesamt fünf Partner miteinander kooperieren und sich abstimmen mussten, machte die Abläufe und Entscheidungsfindungen während der gesamten Projektphase extrem kompliziert.

Ich möchte versuchen, das anhand von zwei Beispielen zu erklären.

Zhou Rong gmp has completed numerous projects in China. Which of gmp's projects in China do you consider to be the most successful, or most representative?

Stephan Schütz It is very difficult to pick out individual projects, because each project has its specific conditions and specific history. Nevertheless, I would like to discuss a project that perfectly reflects the approach of "dialogue in design"—the Chinese National Museum in Beijing.

As you know, we won the project on the strength of a design for an architectural competition that focused heavily on the contrast between the existing building and the extension. A modern roof floating above the existing building was to create a landmark that can be seen from afar, making visible the different time epochs of the creation of the National Museum in the urban context. For an entire year, we refined our competition design in a dialogue with the then clients, until they changed their minds. The previous approach was considered to be inappropriate for the development of the project, because apparently it did not sufficiently honor the historic importance of the square and the existing museum.

As a result, this led to an extension building that seized on the pattern language of the existing building, but in a more abstract, contemporary way. Some elements of the existing building were adopted and transformed so that the history of the building's development becomes apparent for the visitor. This interactive process leads us to fully question our own position. I must add that this is a unique and most likely extreme example in the entire history of the practice. But it also bears witness to the understanding that we, as architects, are not the ones to decide what is built and how, and that our cities and buildings are the result of a collective process. In my view, if an architect applies his or her own individual predetermined style, he or she will be closed to this type of dialogue. I think successful architecture requires an open attitude.

Zhou Rong The China Academy of Building Research (CABR) is one of the most important and traditional architectural institutes in China. The design cooperation between gmp and CABR was a considerable challenge. Both practices had to come to terms with the big differences in the cultural, design, and organizational thinking. Can you perhaps give a few examples of how the two practices communicated with each other during the time of their cooperation?

Ma Lidong First of all, I must say that before the Chinese National Museum project, we had already worked with gmp on fifteen or sixteen projects. But to take this as an example: as already indicated by Stephan Schütz, the extension of the museum is probably gmp's most successful project in China. The same is true for CABR. In my opinion, this success is the result of two things. Firstly, gmp had a very clear objective—this has already been touched on by Stephan Schütz. Secondly, both practices consider communication to be very important. Nevertheless, in this case that was particularly complicated. In normal projects, the communication has to take place between the architects, the client, and the construction company. But in the case of the Chinese National Museum, two more parties were involved: the team of experts and the government team. The team of experts consisted of Wu Liangyong, Zhou Ganzhi, Zhang Jinqiu, Li Daozeng, Peng Yigang, Qi Kang, Ma Guoxin, and others. Representatives of the government included the National Commission for Development and Reform and other authorities. These two additional teams played a decisive role and had a big impact on the project, even more so than in other comparable projects. So the fact that a total of five partners had to cooperate and agree with each other made the processes and decision-making extremely complicated throughout the entire design phase.

I will try to explain this using two examples.

Das erste ist ein fachliches Beispiel. Stephan Schütz hatte über den architektonischen Stil des alten Museums nachgedacht. Was für einen Stil verkörpert das alte Museumsgebäude? Ist es ein konventioneller chinesischer Stil oder doch eher ein europäischer? Selbstverständlich kann man das Gebäude auch als eine Kombination von chinesischem und europäischem Stil beschreiben. Am Eingang des Museums befinden sich zwei Türme, deren Dächer der Form einer mongolischen Jurte ähneln. Andererseits lässt die Gestaltung der Arkaden zwischen diesen beiden Gebäudeteilen Assoziationen an einen klassisch europäischen Stil zu. Wir haben damals viel darüber diskutiert. Dabei habe ich Stephan Schütz von der Entwicklung der chinesischen Architekturgeschichte im vergangenen Jahrhundert erzählt. Zum Beispiel von dem damaligen Einfluss der Sowjetunion auf chinesische Architekten, der Suche nach chinesischen Traditionen oder dem Trend unter chinesischen Studenten, in westlichen Ländern zu studieren und in China dann stark europäisch beeinflusste Architektur zu entwerfen. Vor dem Preisgericht hatte ich das alte Nationalmuseum als eklektizistisch bezeichnet. Daraufhin wurde ich von Kang Qi sofort korrigiert: Das alte Museum sei Klassik.

Zahlreiche solcher Debatten wurden geführt. Dabei ging es gar nicht so sehr darum, dass man Einigung erzielt, zur selben Schlussfolgerung gelangt etc. Wichtig war vielmehr, dass intensiv kommuniziert wurde, denn das führte dazu, dass alle Beteiligten nicht nur einander, sondern auch das Projekt selbst besser verstanden.

Das zweite Beispiel betrifft den Dachvorsprung des neuen Museums. Über dieses Thema haben wir am längsten diskutiert. Viele Detailvorschläge der Architekten wurden im Maßstab 1:1 als Musterstücke angefertigt und begutachtet. Einerseits sollte der Dachvorsprung die chinesische Bautradition widerspiegeln und ausweiten. Gleichzeitig sollte er modern wirken und ganz zu unserer heutigen Zeit passen. Der Dachvorsprung soll die Tradition mit modernen Techniken interpretieren. Darüber debattierten gmp und wir heftig. Wir hatten den Eindruck, dass gmp ein Problem mit dem Dekorativen, dem Ornamentalen hatte, denn das Büro hält einen ganzheitlichen Entwurf, in dem Konstruktion, Material, Funktion und Ästhetik zusammenspielen, für sehr wichtig. Nach zahlreichen Diskussionen zwischen dem Museumsdirektor Lu Zhangshen, CABR, und gmp haben wir schlussendlich doch zusammengefunden. …

Stephan Schütz Die Architektur der Dächer bestimmt die Anmutung aller Bauten in der Verbotenen Stadt und um den Tiananmen-Platz. Das Dach ist ganz generell das Königselement der chinesischen Architektur – deshalb haben die Architekten aller Gebäude am Tiananmen-Platz versucht, die gestaffelten Dächer der Verbotenen Stadt in eine zeitgemäße Form zu übersetzen. Sie haben dies auf sehr direktem Weg getan, indem sie zum Beispiel das Material der glasierten Dachziegel der Verbotenen Stadt inklusive ihrer Farbgebung schlichtweg übernehmen. Im Unterschied dazu wollten wir beim Erweiterungsbau des Nationalmuseums deutlich machen, dass es sich eben nicht um eine traditionelle Dachkonstruktion handelt, schon allein aufgrund der Tatsache, dass unsere Dächer aus Stahl und nicht wie in der Verbotenen Stadt aus Holz konstruiert sind. Hinzu kommt, dass in den gestaffelten Dächern des Neubaus eine Vielzahl technischer Elemente stecken. Dieser Tatbestand führte zu einer technisch anmutenden Erscheinung der Dächer mit ihren bronzenen Metalltafeln und horizontalen Lamellen. Unser Bestreben war es, Tradition und zeitgemäße Anforderungen in einer neuen Dacharchitektur zusammenzubringen.

Zhou Rong Deutschland gilt als einer der Geburtsorte der modernen Architektur. „Moderne Architektur" – das ist in China jedoch ganz lange ein Fremdwort gewesen. Spielt das Wesen der modernen Architektur – so schwer das zu definieren sein mag – bei der Entwurfsphilosophie von gmp eine Rolle?

Stephan Schütz Unter moderner Architektur verstehe ich in erster Linie eine Korrespondenz von Zweck und Form. Deshalb entwerfen wir unsere Architektur entlang der Anforderungen, die aus der Zweckbestimmung eines Bauwerks hervorgehen. Aus der maximalen Reduzierung der angewandten architektonischen Mittel entsteht die ästhetische Qualität unserer Bauwerke. Dies kann jedoch kein Selbstzweck sein!

Es geht vielmehr darum, Räume zu schaffen, die von Menschen benutzt werden und in denen Menschen sich wohlfühlen. Und so haben wir in fast allen Projekten die eigentliche Aufgabenstellung dahingehend erweitert, dass wir auch ein möglichst großes und vielfältiges Angebot von öffentlichen oder halböffentlichen Räumen schaffen, in denen sich Menschen

The first example relates to the architectural style. Stephan Schütz had thought much about the architectural style of the old museum. What style does the old museum building represent? Is it a conventional Chinese style, or rather more a European one? Of course, one can also describe the building as a combination of Chinese and European styles. At the entrance of the museum there are two towers, the roofs of which resemble that of a Mongolian yurt. On the other hand, the design of the arcades between these two parts of the building evokes associations of a classic European style. We had lengthy discussions about that at the time. During these discussions, I told Stephan Schütz about the development of Chinese architectural history in the previous century: for example, about the influence of the Soviet Union on Chinese architects at that time, the search for Chinese traditions, and the trend of Chinese students to study in Western countries and then proceed to design architecture with a strong European influence. To the jury, I had referred to the National Museum as an eclectic building. But Kang Qi immediately corrected me: the old museum, he said, represented the classical style.

There were many debates of that kind. The point was not so much that of achieving a consensus, of drawing the same conclusions, etc. Rather, it was important to carry out intensive communication because the result was that all those involved were able to understand each other—and the project—much better.

The second example is about the roof projection for the new museum. This was the subject that was discussed the longest. Many detailed proposals by the architects were produced as 1:1 scale models and assessed. On the one hand, the roof projection was supposed to reflect and expand on the Chinese building tradition. At the same time, it was to appear modern and contemporary in all respects. The idea of the roof projection is to interpret tradition with modern methods. This issue was one of intense debate between gmp and us. We were under the impression that gmp had a problem with decorative elements, with ornamental patterns, because the practice considers a holistic design—in which construction, materials, function and aesthetics all interact—as very important.

After numerous discussions between the museum's Director, Lu Zhangshen, CABR, and gmp, we finally found common ground I think that Stephan Schütz may also be able to say a few words about that...

Stephan Schütz   The architecture of the roofs has a big influence on the appearance of all buildings in the Forbidden City and around Tiananmen Square. Generally speaking, the roof is the royal element of Chinese architecture, which is why the architects of all buildings at Tiananmen Square have tried to translate the staggered roofs of the Forbidden City into a contemporary form. They have done this in a very direct way, for example by simply adopting the same material of the Forbidden City's glazed roof tiles, including the color. By contrast, we wanted to make it clear in the extension to the National Museum that the roof construction was not a traditional one, if only for the fact that our roofs are made of steel and not of timber as in the Forbidden City. Furthermore, there is the fact that the staggered roofs of the new building accommodate numerous technical elements. This gave the roofs a technical appearance, with their bronze-colored metal plates and slat-like horizontal elements. We tried to bring together traditional and contemporary requirements in a new type of roof architecture.

Zhou Rong   Germany is considered to be one of the birthplaces of modern architecture. But the term "modern architecture" has been a foreign phrase in China for a very long time. Does the essence of modern architecture—however difficult that may be to define—play an important role in gmp's design philosophy?

Stephan Schütz   For me, modern architecture is primarily an interaction between purpose and form. For this reason, we design our architecture according to the detailed requirements that result from the overall purpose of the building. The aesthetic quality of our buildings develops from reducing stylistic means to those architectural elements required in the construction. However this cannot be a purpose in itself!

begegnen können und angenehme Bedingungen für zwischenmenschlichen Austausch vorfinden. Diese Räume können unterschiedliche Dimensionen und Bedeutung haben, wie zum Beispiel das Grand Forum im Nationalmuseum, die Platzräume unterhalb der Dächer in der Oper in Qingdao oder Tianjin, oder die großen Hallenräume und Galerien in unseren Bürogebäuden. Diese Räume waren nicht selbstverständlicher Teil der Aufgabe. Sie sind Zusätze, die aber die Qualität der Projekte zu einem wesentlichen Teil bestimmen.

Zhou Rong   Herr Ma, inwieweit unterscheiden sich die Auffassungen deutscher und chinesischer Architekten in Bezug auf die „Moderne Architektur"?

Ma Lidong   Meiner Meinung nach werden die chinesischen Architekten stärker von der politischen Umgebung oder von den Bauherren selbst beeinflusst. Das hindert viele chinesische Architekten daran, auf ein höheres Niveau zu kommen. Nur: Wenn sie das nicht erreichen, dann wird es schwierig, eine eigene Entwurfsidee zu entwickeln und einen eigenständigen Charakter zu präsentieren. Natürlich haben die chinesischen Architekten die Verantwortung, die chinesische Tradition und die damit verbundenen kulturellen Erkenntnisse zu erweitern. Gleichzeitig müssen sie aber in ihrer Kreativität auf der Höhe der Zeit sein. Im Moment versuchen sie sich noch zu orientieren; noch gibt es keine richtige Balance zwischen diesen beiden Polen. Zweifellos können deutsche Architekten, wie zum Beispiel gmp, im Vergleich zu chinesischen den Begriff der „Modernen Architektur" besser verstehen und interpretieren. Einem Büro wie gmp fällt es viel leichter, das Verhältnis zwischen Geschichte und moderner Kreativität zu reflektieren – und das Ergebnis dieser Reflexion praktisch umzusetzen. Dank seiner Erfahrung und Kompetenz kann gmp mit Raum, Form und Material nach eigenen Prinzipien verfahren. Das Beharren auf der Entwurfsidee von gmp war daher der Schlüssel zum Erfolg.

Zhou Rong   Herr Schütz, wie beurteilen Sie die zeitgenössische deutsche Architektur – und die Möglichkeiten des Austauschs zwischen deutscher und chinesischer Architektur?

Stephan Schütz   Wie gesagt, die Situation für deutsche Architekten ist konträr zu der unserer Kollegen in China. In Deutschland gilt es auszuloten, wie man vorhandene Ressourcen in der Stadt nutzen und umwandeln kann, wie man nachhaltige Gebäude bauen sollte. Ich glaube, dass in diesem Thema ein Potenzial des deutsch-chinesischen Austausches auf dem Feld der Architektur in den nächsten Jahren liegen wird.

Wie kann man aus dem Vorhandenen Infrastrukturen mit entsprechender Dauerhaftigkeit schaffen? Die Frage, wie Tradition und Moderne zusammenwirken können, wird sich in China immer weniger auf bauliche Symbolik und Metaphorik fokussieren, sondern auf die Nutzbarmachung des ohnehin Vorhandenen.

Zhou Rong   Herr Ma, Sie haben über 20 Projekte in Zusammenarbeit mit gmp realisiert. Welche Erfahrungen haben Sie dabei gesammelt?

Ma Lidong   Da sind vor allem zwei Erfahrungen zu nennen. Die eine hat mit dem „Dialogischen Entwerfen" zu tun. Davon haben wir alle – unser Büroteam und ich selbst auch – sehr viel gelernt. Zum Beispiel, dass man auf der einen Seite während der Planungs- und Realisierungsphase eines Projektes dem Entwurfskonzept treu bleiben und auf dessen hochqualitativer Umsetzung bestehen muss. Andererseits muss man für Vorschläge von allen Seiten offen bleiben. Aber bis ein Konsens aller Meinungen gefunden ist, sollte man prinzipiell auf dem Entwurfskonzept bestehen. Zu lernen, wie gut es ist, wenn ein Architekturbüro auf diese Weise arbeitet – das war eine sehr positive Erfahrung. Denn chinesische Architekten geraten allzu oft in zwei extreme Positionen: Entweder verhalten sie sich zu dickköpfig und störrisch, oder sie tun das Gegenteil und gehen viel zu viele und viel zu faule Kompromisse ein. Ein solches Verhalten ist unverantwortlich, weil es sowohl dem Bauherrn als auch dem Architekten selbst schadet. Eine gute, effektive Kommunikation hingegen bietet die Möglichkeit, die Entwurfsidee des Architekten wie geplant zu realisieren und die Vorstellungen des Bauherrn in diesen Prozess zu integrieren.

It is our objective to create spaces that are used by people and where people feel at home. This is why we have extended the original briefing in almost all projects to the effect that we also create as large and diverse a range of public and semipublic spaces as possible, where people can meet and find agreeable conditions for human interaction. These spaces can have different dimensions and meaning, such as the Grand Forum in the National Museum, the spaces beneath the roofs of the opera houses in Qingdao or Tianjin, or the large forums and galleries in our office buildings. These spaces were not an original part of the briefing. They are additions, but they are additions which—to a large extent—determine the quality of the project.

Zhou Rong   Mr. Ma, how does the understanding of "modern architecture" differ between German and Chinese architects?

Ma Lidong   I feel that Chinese architects are more influenced by their political environment or the building owners. This is an impediment to many Chinese architects in reaching a higher level. But if they do not reach that, then it becomes difficult to develop their own design idea and present an independent style. Of course, Chinese architects have the responsibility to extend Chinese tradition and to expand the cultural understanding associated with it. At the same time, in terms of their creativity, they need to keep abreast of modern developments. At this point in time, they are still trying to find their way; there is not yet a proper balance between the two extremes. I have no doubt that German architects, such as those from gmp, can better understand and interpret the term "modern architecture" than their Chinese colleagues. For a practice such as gmp, it is much easier to reflect upon the relationship between history and modern creativity, and to put the result of this reflection into practice. Thanks to its experience and competence, gmp can apply its own principles with respect to space, form, and material. Therefore, gmp's insistence on their design idea was the key to success.

Zhou Rong   Mr. Schütz, how do you assess contemporary German architecture and the possibility of an exchange between German and Chinese architecture?

Stephan Schütz   As I have said before, the situation faced by German architects is quite different to that of our colleagues in China. In Germany, we are faced with the task of finding out how existing resources in the city can be used and converted, and how sustainable buildings should be built. I believe that in the field of architecture, there is potential for a German/Chinese exchange regarding this subject in the years to come. How is it possible to create infrastructure buildings with appropriate long-term function on the basis of what is existing? The question as to how tradition and the Moderne can interact in China will focus less and less on symbolism and metaphors in buildings, and instead on making use of what already exists.

Zhou Rong   Mr. Ma, you have completed over twenty projects in cooperation with gmp. What experience have you gained?

Ma Lidong   There are mainly two aspects I would like to mention. The first has to do with "dialogue in design." We all have learned a lot from that—our practice team, and I myself too. For example, that—on the one hand—one must keep one's faith in the design concept during the design and implementation phase, and one must insist on its high-quality implementation. On the other hand, one has to remain open to proposals from all sides. But until a consensus of all opinions has been found, one should insist on the design concept as a matter of principle. To learn how good it is when an architectural practice works in this way – that was a very positive experience. Because Chinese architects all too often adopt one of two extreme positions: they are either too stubborn and headstrong, or they do the opposite and make far too many poor compromises. Such behavior is not responsible, because it is detrimental to both the building owner and the architects themselves. By contrast, good and effective communication offers the opportunity to implement the architect's design idea as planned, and to integrate the building owner's ideas during this process.

Die andere wesentliche Erfahrung betrifft die Professionalisierung der Planungsverfahren. Wenn man auf die Geschichte unserer Büro-Kooperationen schaut, lassen sich drei Epochen unterscheiden. Die erste Epoche markiert die Zusammenarbeit mit deutschen Architekten für das Projekt „Lufthansa Center in Peking", in den 80er Jahren. Die zweite die Kooperation mit I.M. Pei für den „Bank of China Tower" in den 90ern. Und die dritte Epoche wurde geprägt durch die Zusammenarbeit mit gmp für die Erweiterung des chinesischen Nationalmuseums.

Allen drei Projekten ist die ganzheitliche Planung unter Leitung der Architekten gemeinsam. In allen Fällen war sie die Voraussetzung dafür, dass am Ende die hohen Ansprüche an Funktion, Technik und Ästhetik eingelöst werden konnten.

Aber die Dimension des Planungsverfahrens für das Museum war noch einmal etwas anderes. Ich habe es eben schon erwähnt: Nicht nur kamen alle Abteilungen unseres Büros für dieses Projekt zum Einsatz, sondern es kamen noch die Fachteams der Staatsinstitute dazu, Gründungstechnik-Experten, zum Beispiel Fachleute für Konstruktionen mit großer Spannweite, Brandschutzexperten und so weiter. Nur die Zusammenarbeit so vieler Fachleute konnte gewährleisten, dass das Projekt in dieser Qualität realisiert werden konnte, in funktioneller, technischer, ästhetischer und nicht zuletzt wirtschaftlicher Hinsicht. Und das hat jeden unserer Mitarbeiter besonders motiviert, sich einzubringen.

Zhou Rong Herr Schütz, wie schätzen Sie die Zukunft von gmp in China ein?

Stephan Schütz Aufgrund der sich auch in China verändernden wirtschaftlichen Verhältnisse werden sich rationalere Denkmodelle ausbreiten, die weniger der Demonstration von Bedeutung und Wirtschaftskraft dienen, sondern vielmehr den individuellen Bedürfnissen der Menschen entsprechen. Ich glaube, dass die Zeit der großen Symbolprojekte zu Ende gehen wird. Diese Hinwendung zu einer rationalen Architektur, die die gewaltigen Probleme der Umwelt ebenso aufgreift wie das allerorten spürbare Bedürfnis, öffentliche Räume zu schaffen, in denen sich Menschen wohlfühlen, ist eine große Herausforderung, bei der gmp seinen Beitrag leisten wird.

Wir glauben daran, dass gmp in China eine erfolgreiche Zukunft hat. Wir hoffen, dass wir in Zusammenarbeit mit chinesischen Kollegen noch viele interessante Architekturprojekte realisieren können, die mit gesellschaftlicher Verantwortung, ästhetischem Anspruch und Nachhaltigkeit die Baukultur dieses Landes prägen.

The other important experience concerns the professionalism of the design processes. When you look back over the history of our practice cooperation, you can identify three distinct phases. The first phase is that of the cooperation with German architects on the Lufthansa Center in Beijing project in the 1980s. The second is the cooperation with I.M. Pei on the Bank of China Tower in the 1990s. And the third phase was characterized by the cooperation with gmp on the extension of the Chinese National Museum.

All three projects have in common the holistic design approach under the leadership of the architects. In all cases, this was the prerequisite for being able to satisfy the demanding brief with respect to function, technology and aesthetics.

But the complexity of the design process for the museum was yet another level of experience. I've mentioned it already: this project required not only the involvement of all departments in our practice, but also the specialist teams of the State Institute, foundation experts, structural experts for the construction of large spans, fire safety experts, etc. The cooperation of all these experts was needed to ensure that the project could be completed to this high degree of quality in terms of function, technology, aesthetics and—not least —cost efficiency. And that provided extra motivation to all our members of staff to give their very best.

Zhou Rong   Mr. Schütz, how do you assess the gmp's future in China?

Stephan Schütz   Owing to the economic conditions— which are also changing in China—more rational approaches will gain ground, which are less focused on the demonstration of importance and commercial power, and more on the actual requirements of the people. I believe that the time of large, symbolic projects will come to an end. This move towards a rational architecture, which tackles the enormous environmental problems, as well as the ubiquitous desire to create public spaces where people feel at their ease, is a great challenge in which gmp will make its contribution.

We believe that gmp will have a successful future in China. We hope that—in cooperation with Chinese colleagues—we will be able to complete many interesting architectural projects that will contribute to shaping the architecture of this country in a socially responsible way, which is both sustainable and aesthetically pleasing.

Fotomontage zum Entwurf des Chinesischen Nationalmuseums am Platz des Himmlischen Friedens, vis à vis die Große Halle des Volkes, im Hintergrund die Verbotene Stadt.
Photomontage of the National Museum of China situated at the Tiananmen Square, opposite the Great Hall of the People, in the background of the Forbidden City.

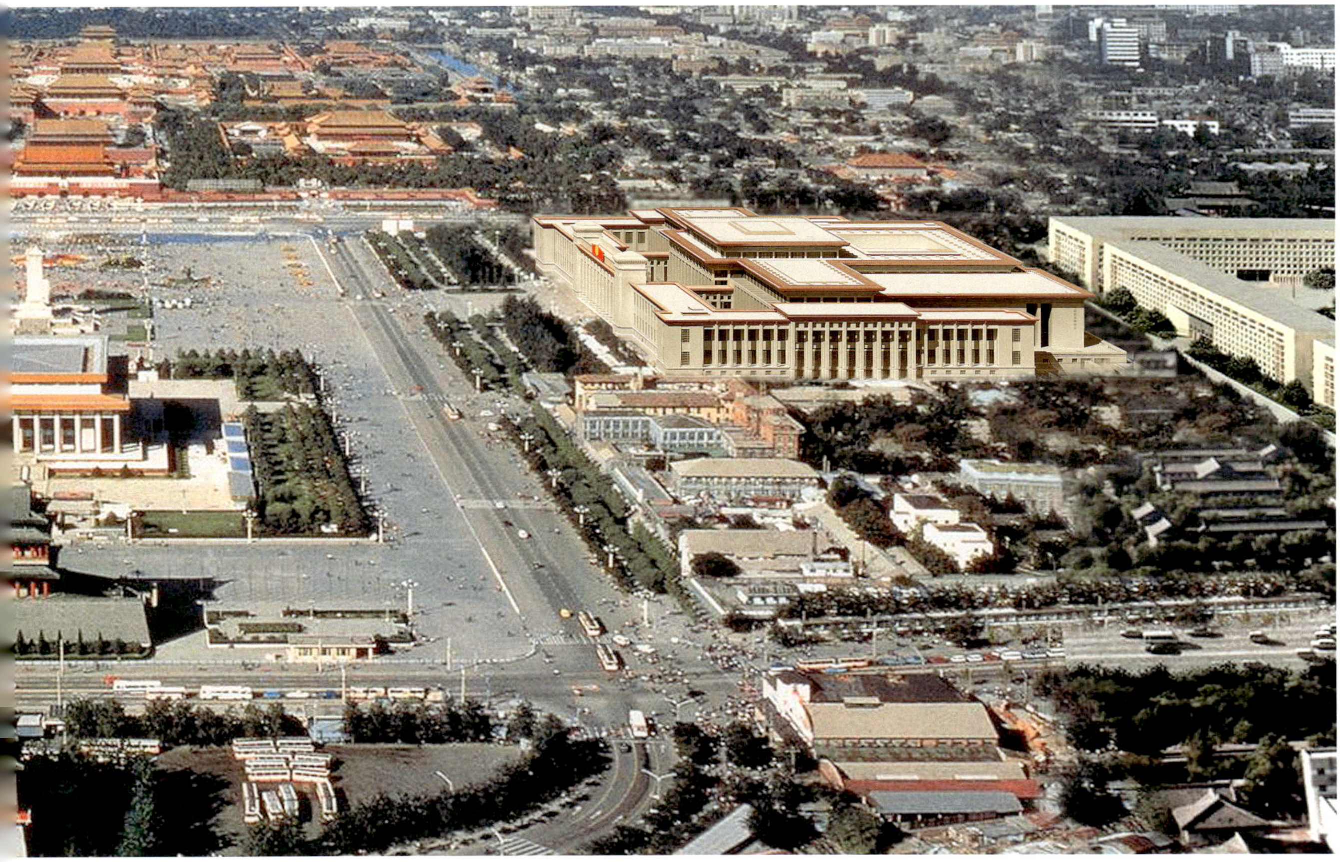

Westansicht
West elevation

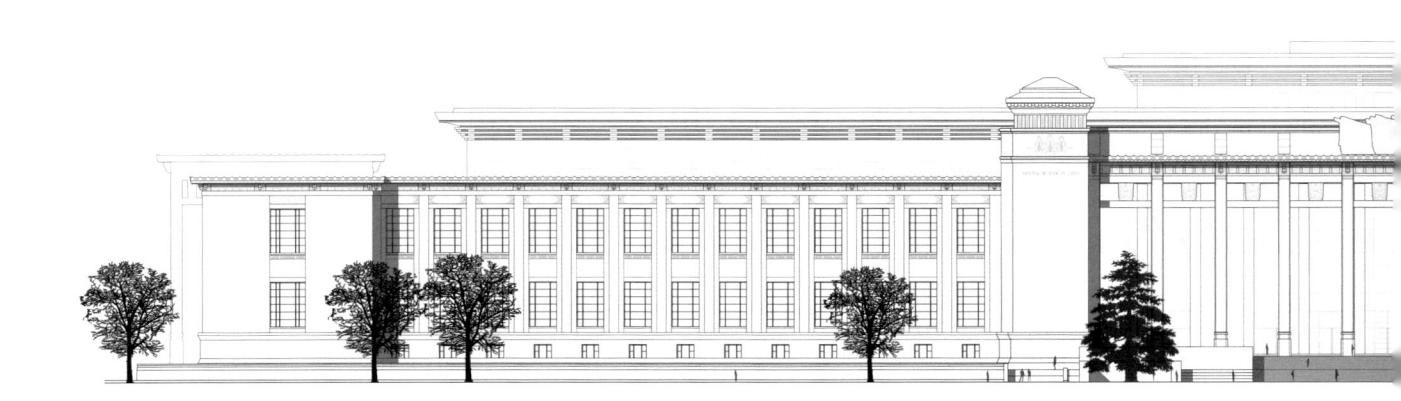

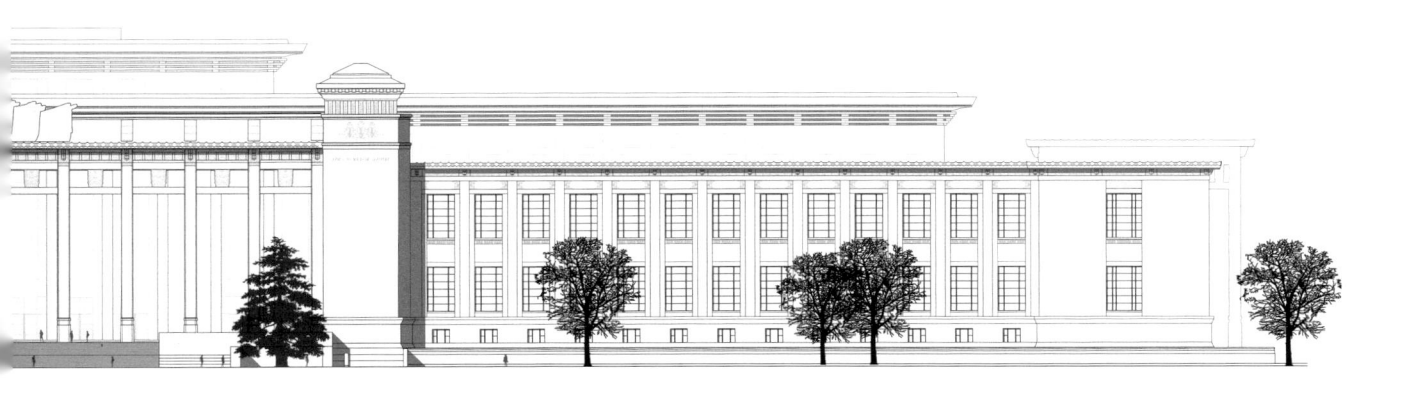

THE NATIONAL MUSEUM OF CHINA Plans and Drawings

0 5 10   20   50m

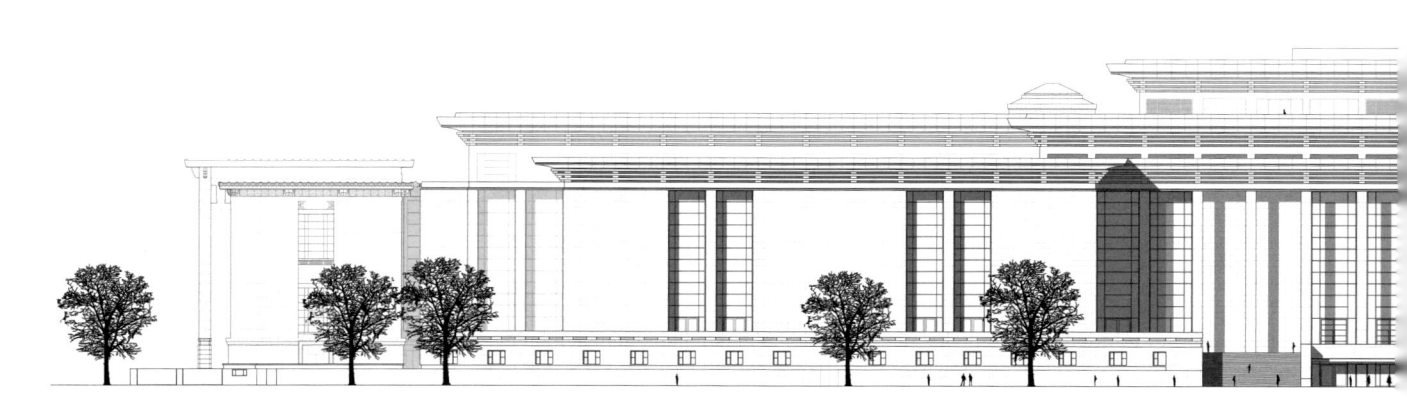

52 DAS CHINESISCHE NATIONALMUSEUM   Pläne und Zeichnungen

Ostansicht
East elevation

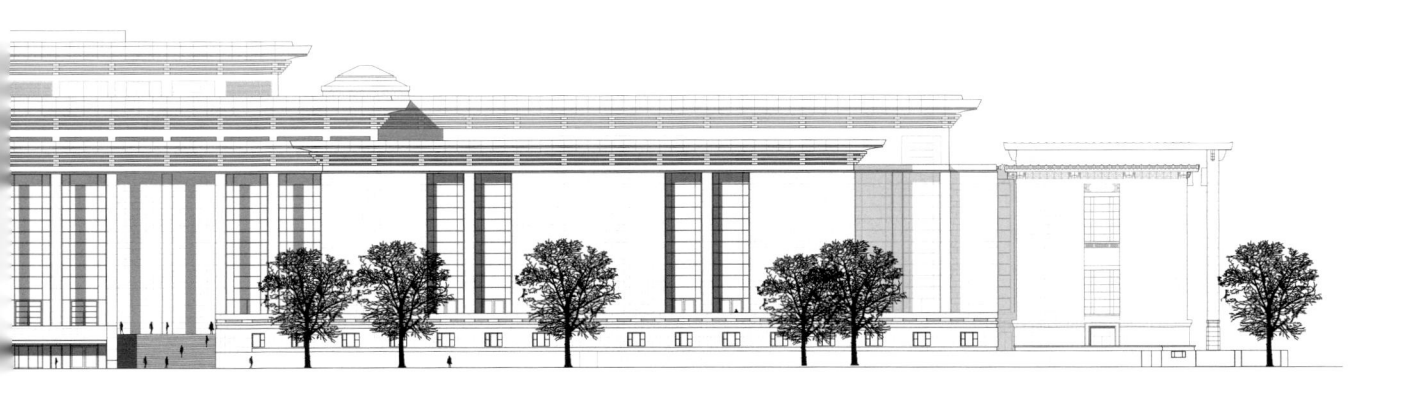

THE NATIONAL MUSEUM OF CHINA Plans and Drawings

0 5 10   20   50m

0 5 10   20   50m

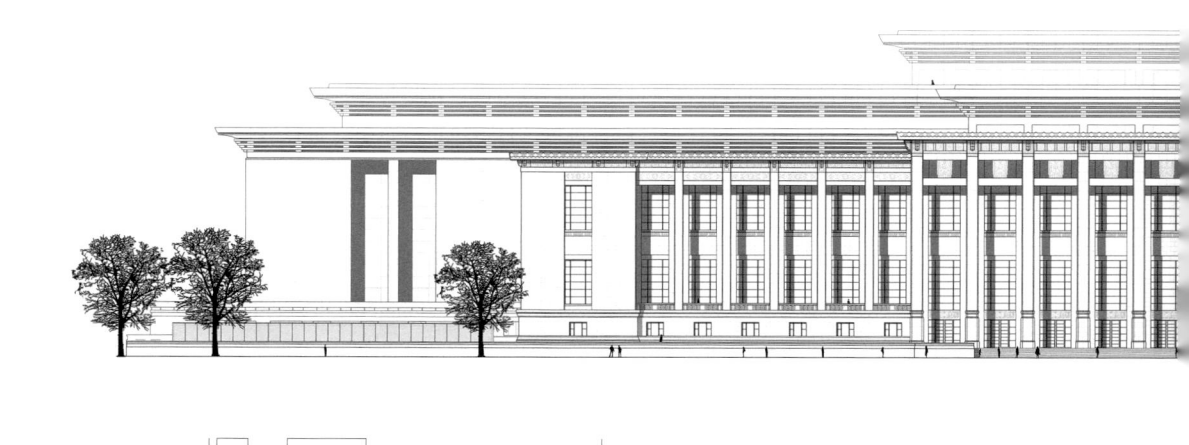

Nordansicht
North elevation

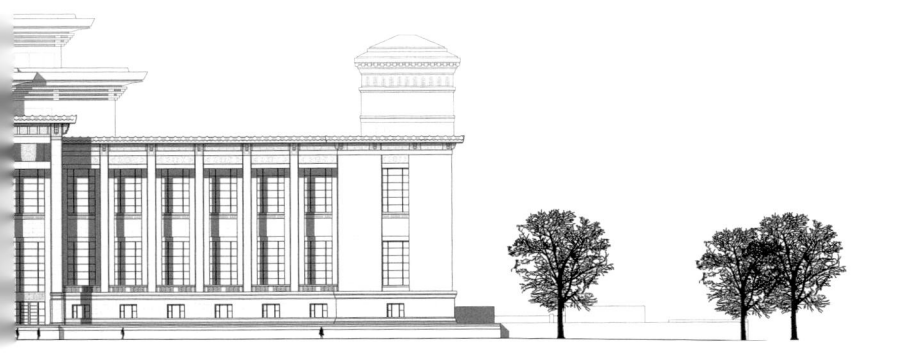

THE NATIONAL MUSEUM OF CHINA Plans and Drawings

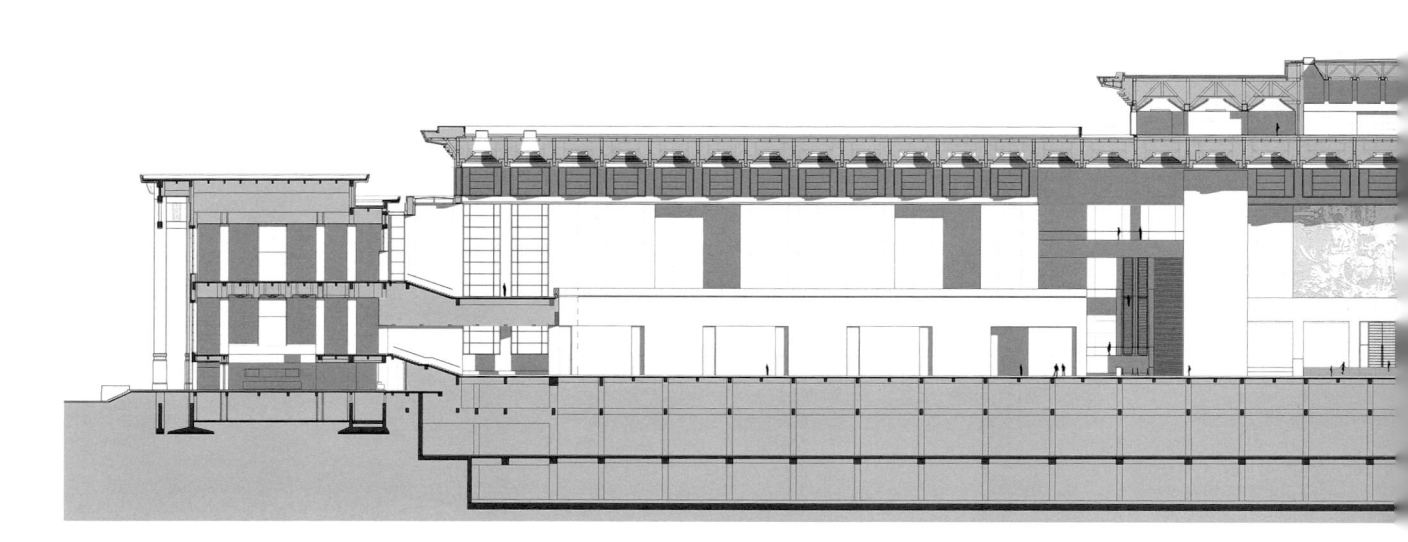

56 DAS CHINESISCHE NATIONALMUSEUM   Pläne und Zeichnungen

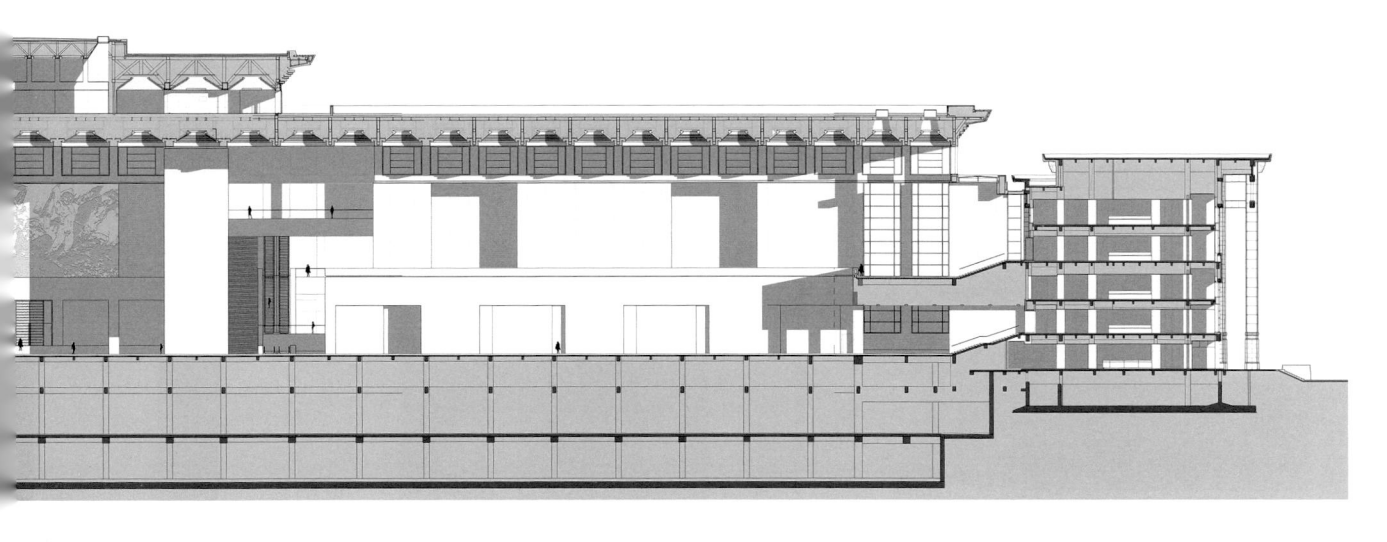

THE NATIONAL MUSEUM OF CHINA Plans and Drawings

0 5 10   20   50m

Längsschnitt durch das Forum
Forum: Longitudinal section

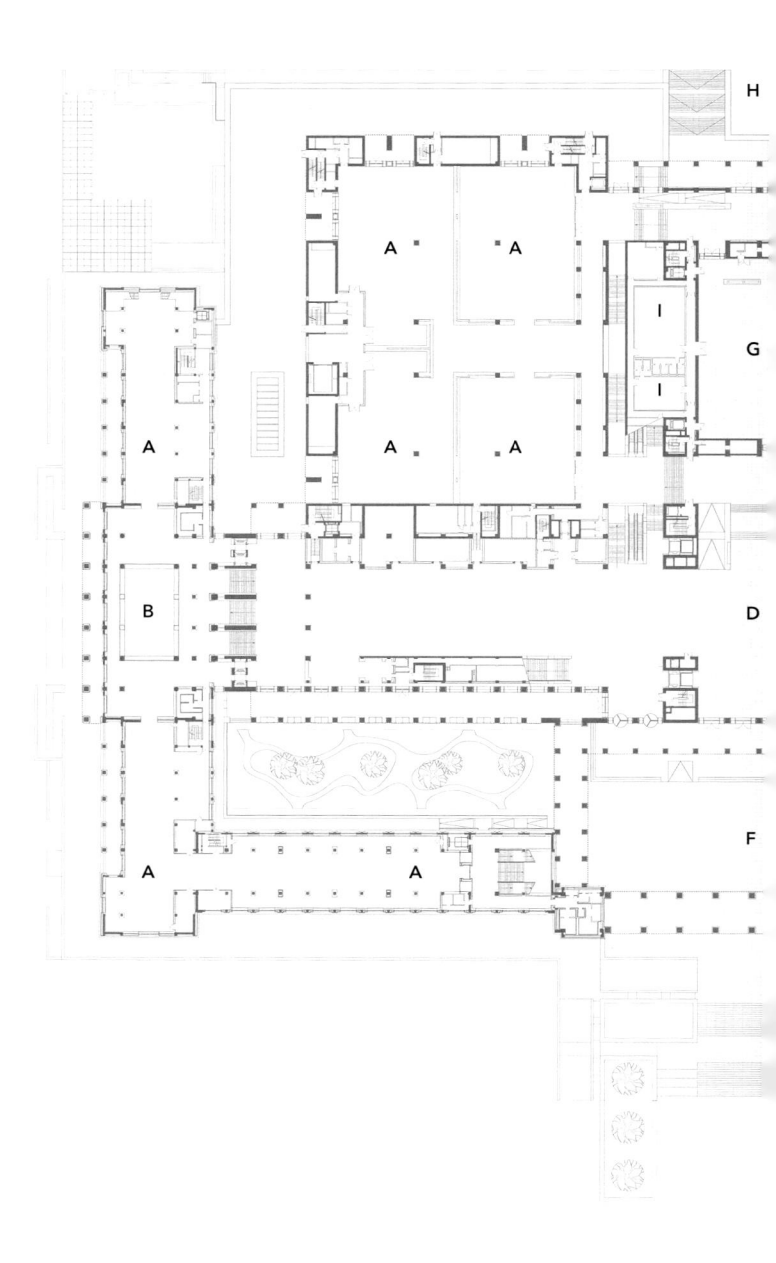

↑ Grundriss Hauptebene – Forum,
Haupteingang, Eingangsebene West
Floor plan of Main Level – Forum,
Main Entrance, Entrance Level west
A Ausstellung Exhibition
B Nordfoyer Northern Foyer
C Bibliothek Library

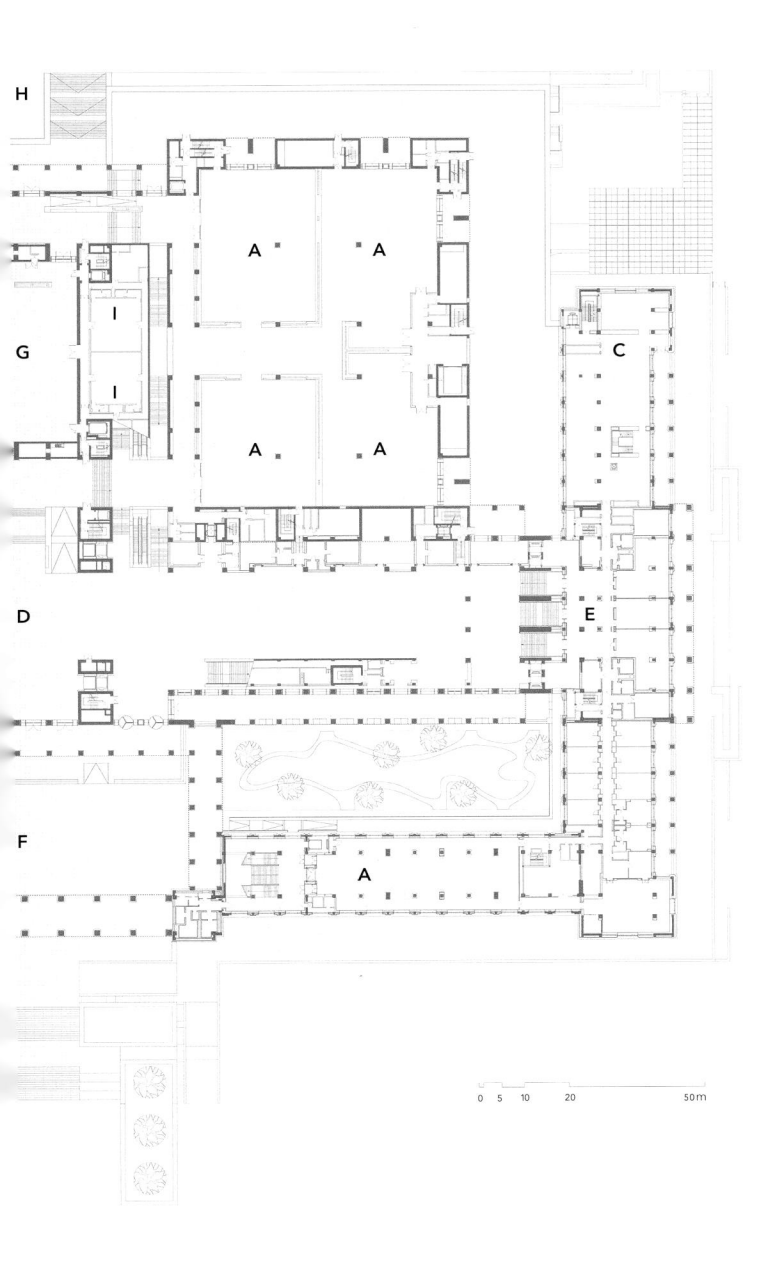

THE NATIONAL MUSEUM OF CHINA Plans and Drawings

D Große Eingangshalle Grand Forum
E Nordfoyer Northern Foyer
F Westlicher Eingangshof Western Entance Courtyard
G Zentrale Halle Central Hall
H Ostfoyer Eastern Foyer
I Empfangsräume Reception Rooms

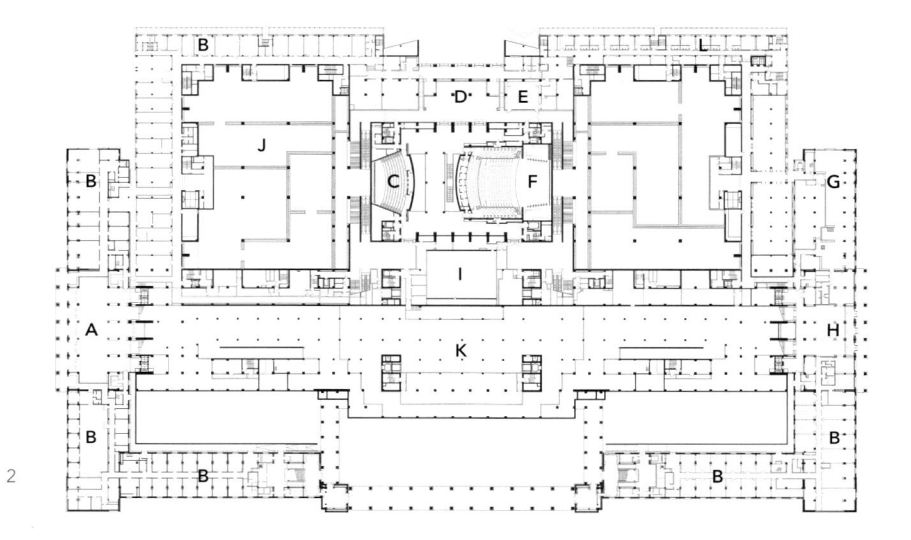

↑ 1
Grundriss Galerieebene
Floor plan Gallery Level
A Ausstellung Exhibition
B Büros Offices
C Gallery Gallery
D Verwaltung Administration

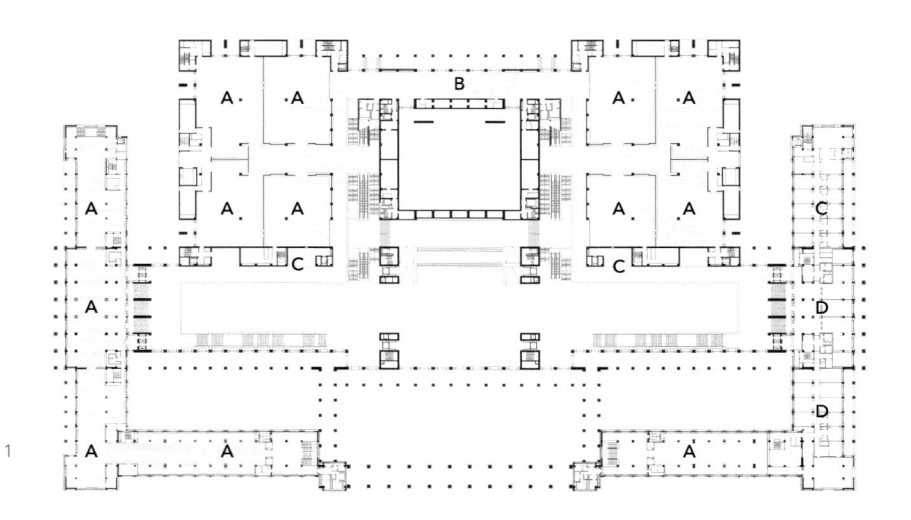

↑ 2
Grundriss Eingangsebene
mit Zugängen auf der
Nord-, Süd- und Ostseite
Floor plan Entrance Level
with access from north,
south and east

A Nordfoyer Northern Foyer
B Bürotrakt Offices
C Hörsaal Auditorium
D Ostfoyer Eastern Foyer
E Presseraum Press Room
F Theater Theater

G Bibliothek Library
H Südfoyer Southern Foyer
I Fernsehstudio TV Studio
J Ausstellung Exhibition
K Parken Parking
L Gästeräume Guest Rooms

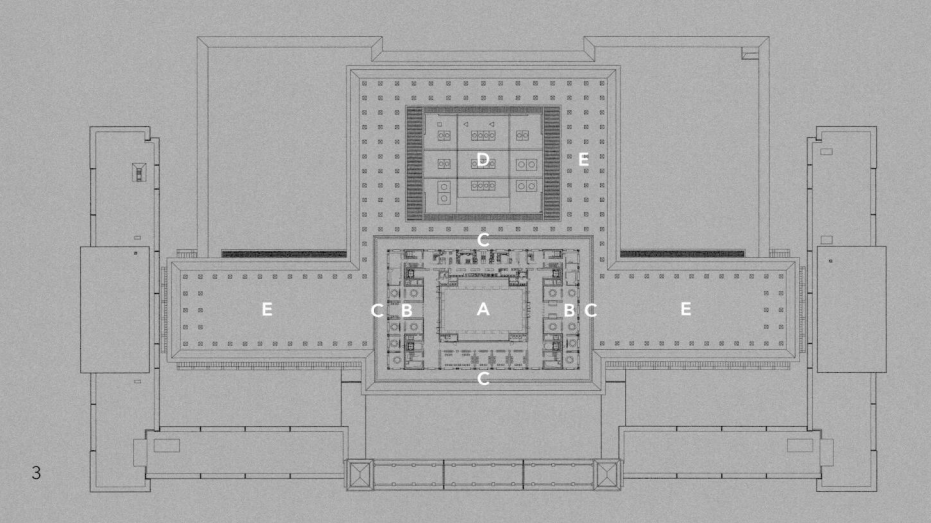

THE NATIONAL MUSEUM OF CHINA   Plans and Drawings

↑ 3
Grundriss Dachebene
Floor Plan Roof Level
A Jade-Halle Jade Hall
B VIP-Restaurant VIP Restaurant
C Dachterrasse Roof Terrace
D Technik (abgesenkt)
   Technical Engineering (lowered)
E Begrüntes Dach Green Roof

Fotografische Dokumentation   Photographic Documentation

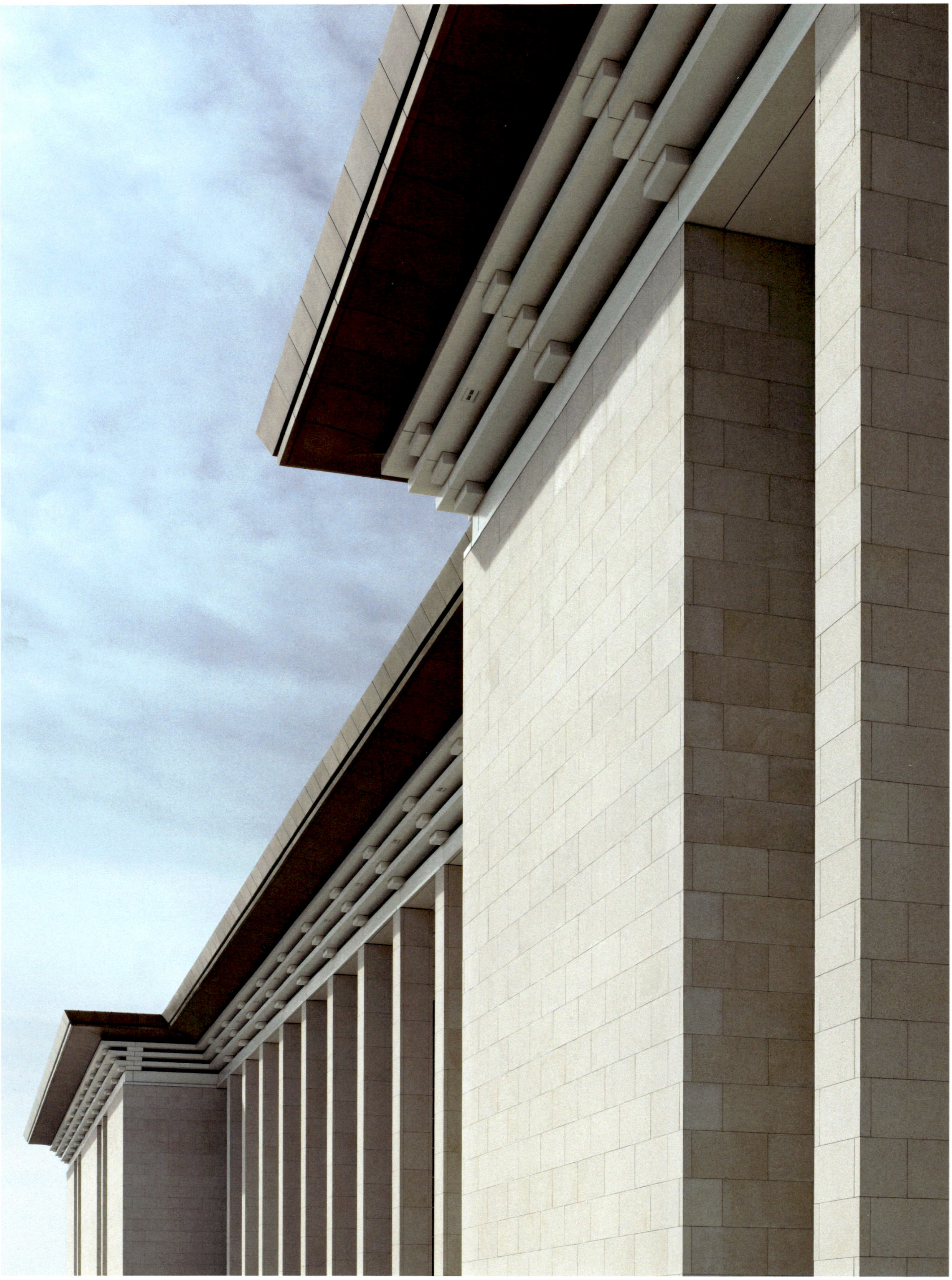

THE NATIONAL MUSEUM OF CHINA Photographic Documentation

↗ Die für den Bestandsbau typischen Kolonnaden und Fensterarchitekturen wurden in eine zeitgemäße Formensprache übersetzt.
The colonnades and window styles—typical of the existing building—were translated into contemporary design vocabulary.
← Detail der Ostfassade
Detail of the eastern façade

→ ▢ Eingangsbereich am Platz des Himmlischen Friedens. Rechts – der Altbau mit den zurückliegenden, gestaffelten Dächern des Neubaus.
Entrance area at the Tiananmen Square. Right side – the building with the inset staggered roofs of the new building.

66 DAS CHINESISCHE NATIONALMUSEUM Fotografische Dokumentation

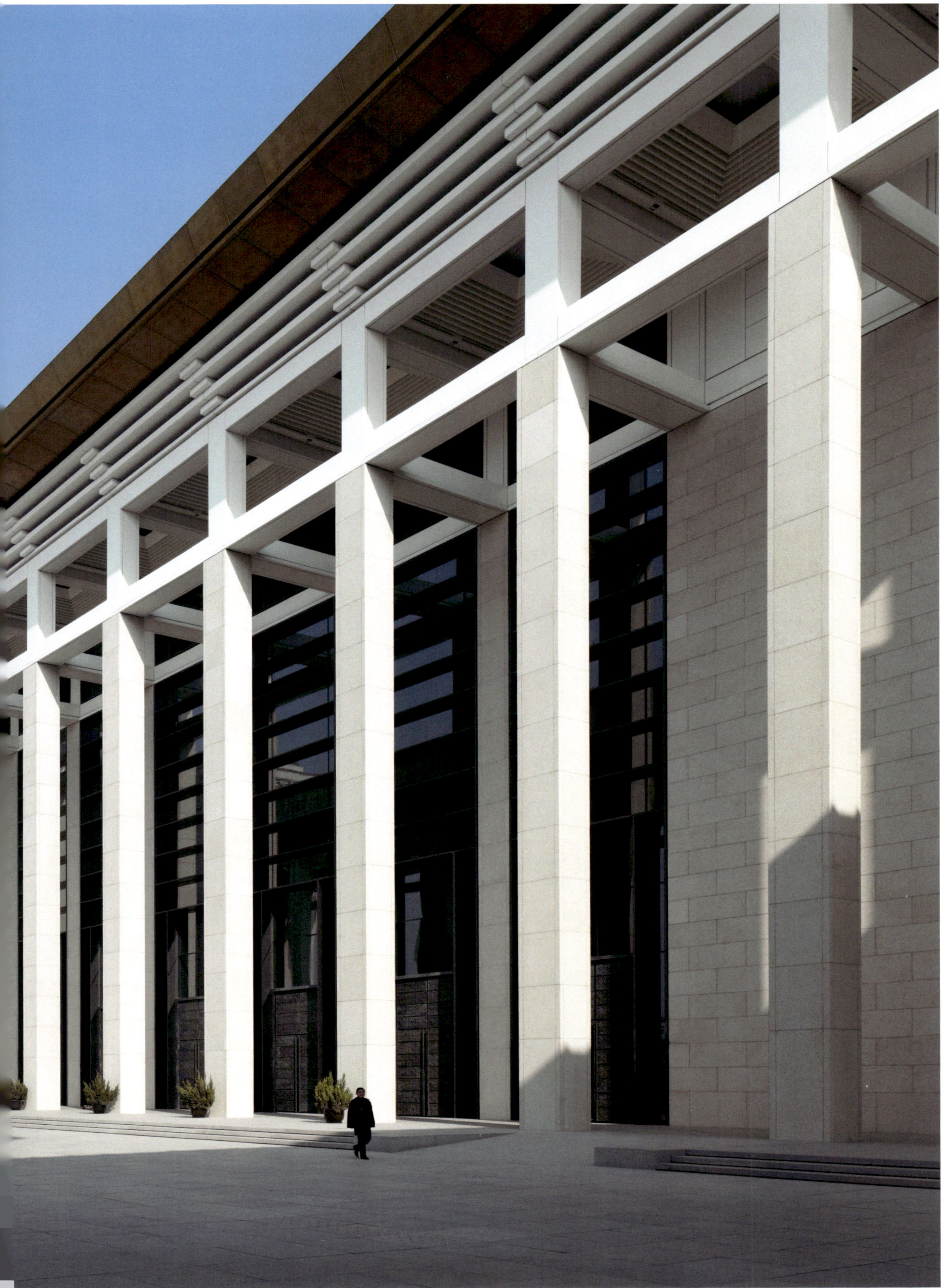

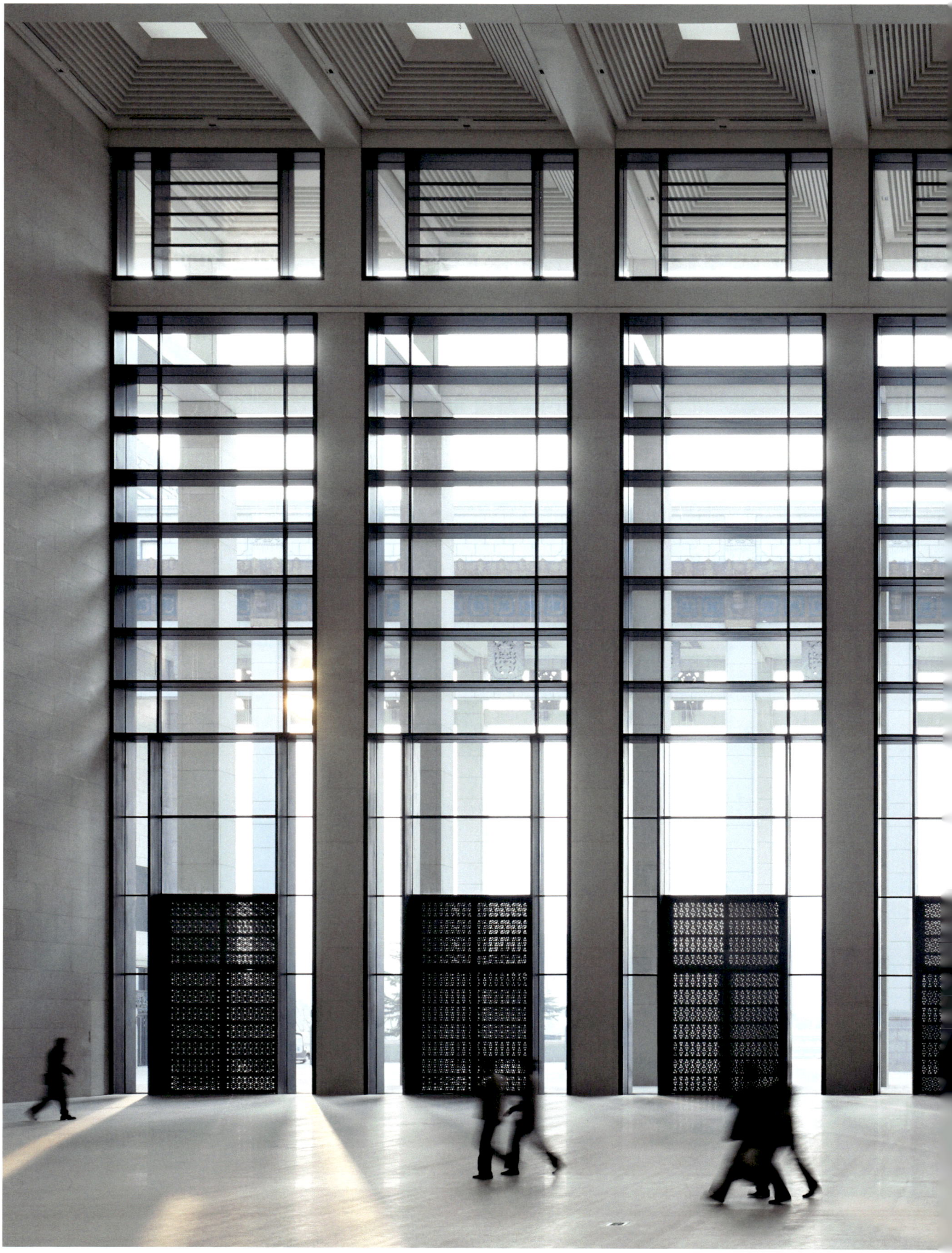

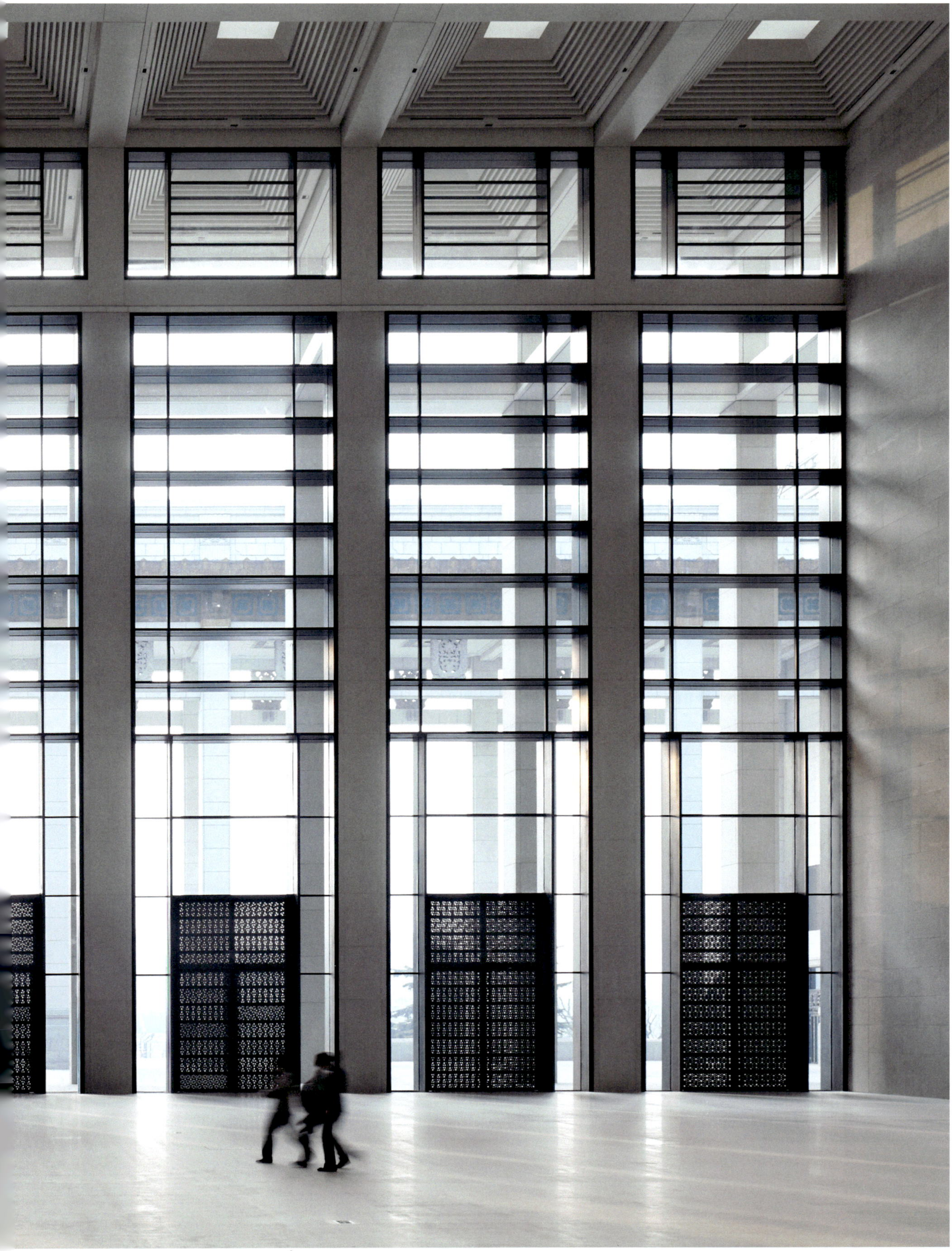

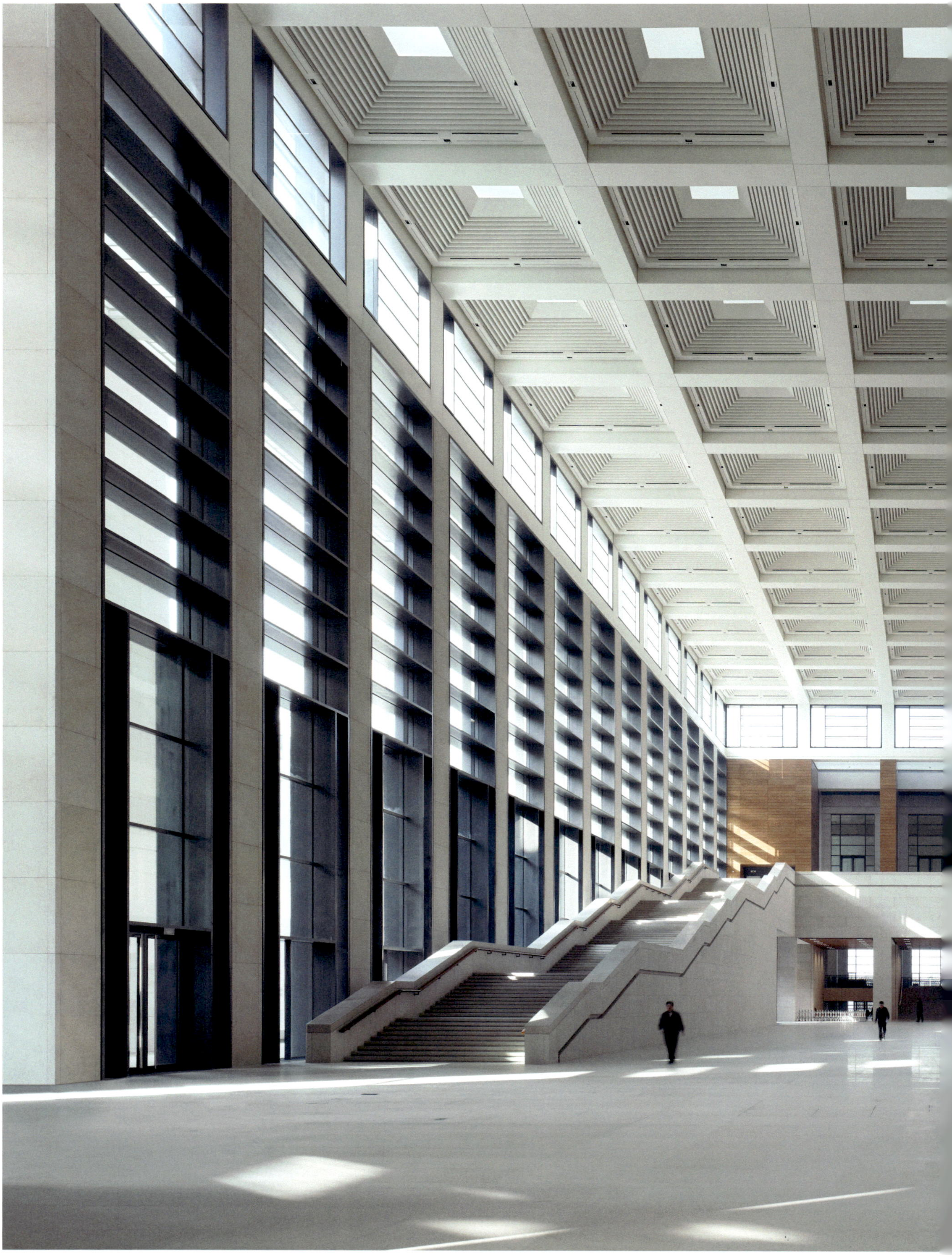

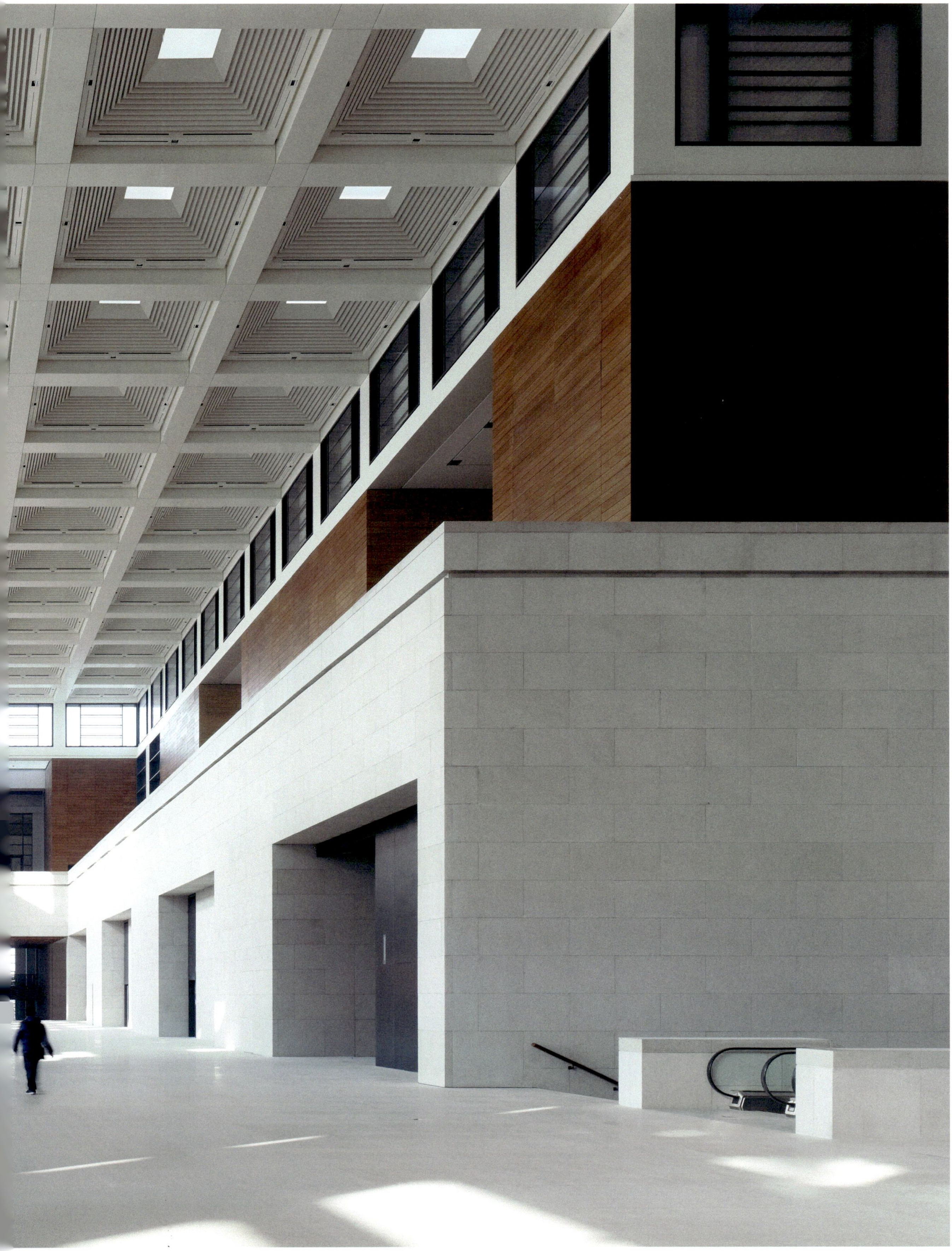

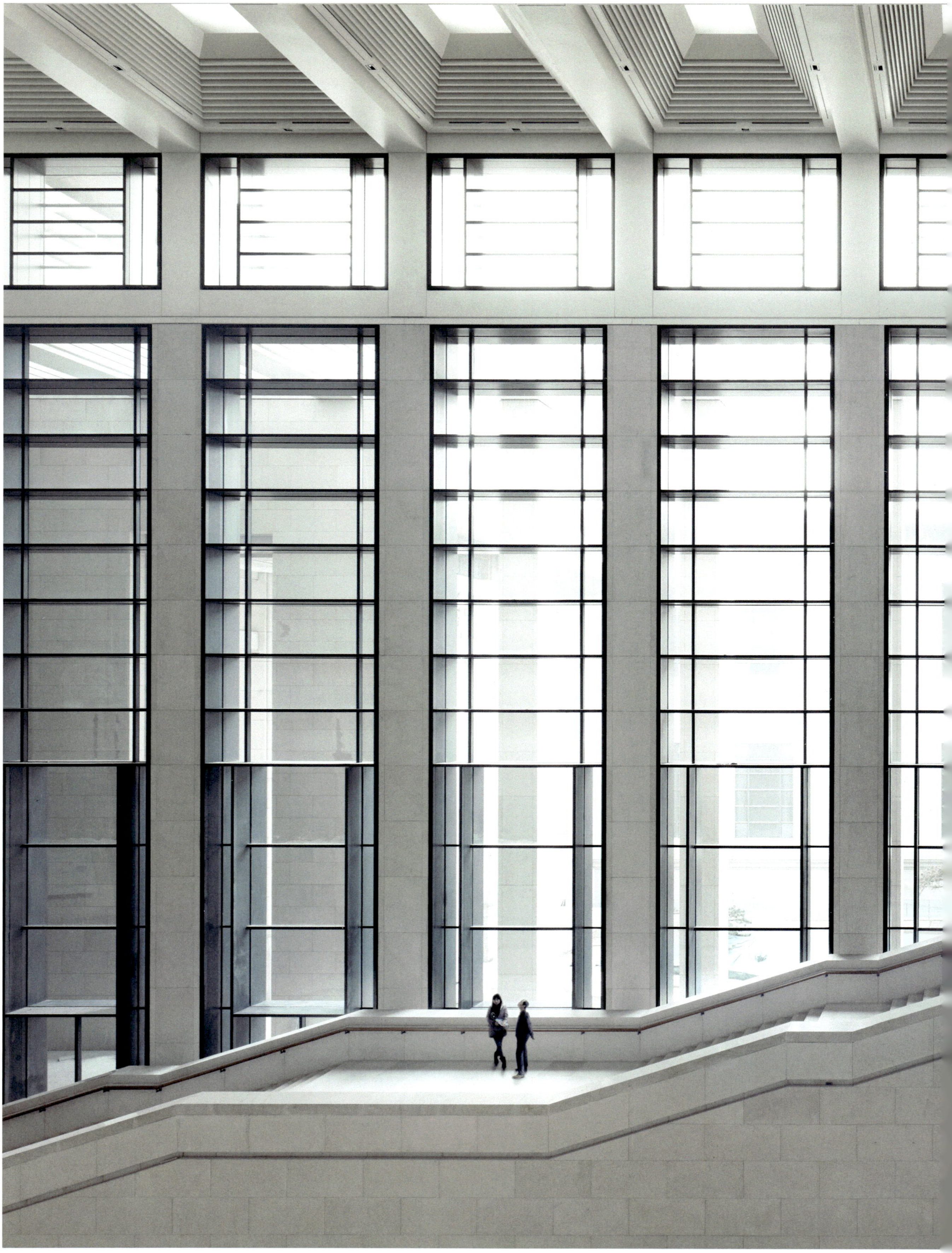

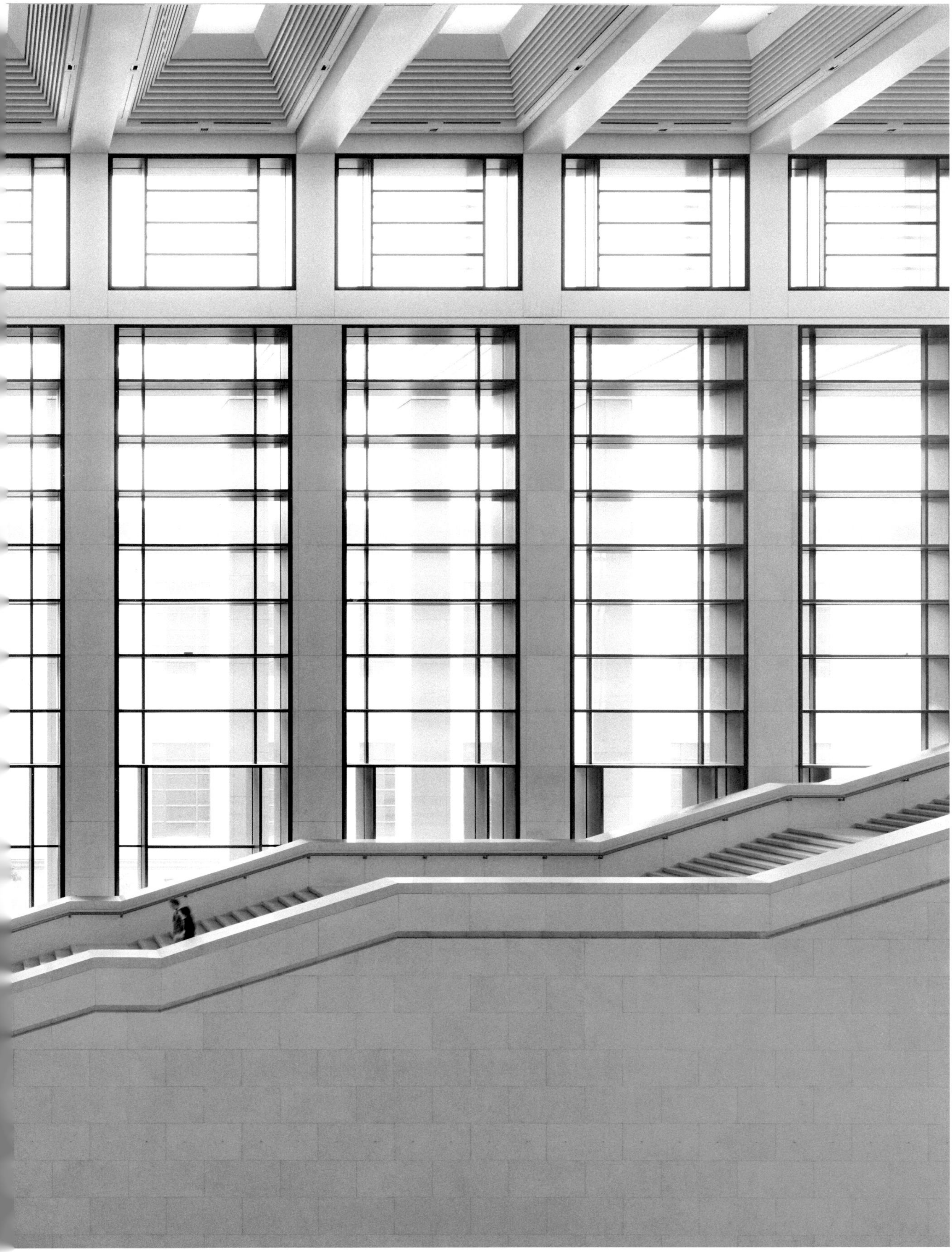

DAS CHINESISCHE NATIONALMUSEUM   Fotografische Dokumentation

←←← ⬜ Im Forum, Blick nach Westen
Western view inside the Forum

←← ⬜ Das Grand Forum umfasst nahezu 9000 Quadratmeter
The Grand Forum is close to 9,000 square meters

← ⬜ Treppenaufgang im Forum
Staircase inside the Forum

THE NATIONAL MUSEUM OF CHINA Photographic Documentation

↑ Mit rotem Stoff bespannte
Wände in der zentralen Halle
The walls of the Central Hall
are covered with red fabric.

↑ → Das Forum bietet den Besuchern Orientierung, alle öffentlichen Bereiche werden von diesem Raum aus erschlossen.
The Forum helps visitors with orientation; all public areas of the building are accessible from here.

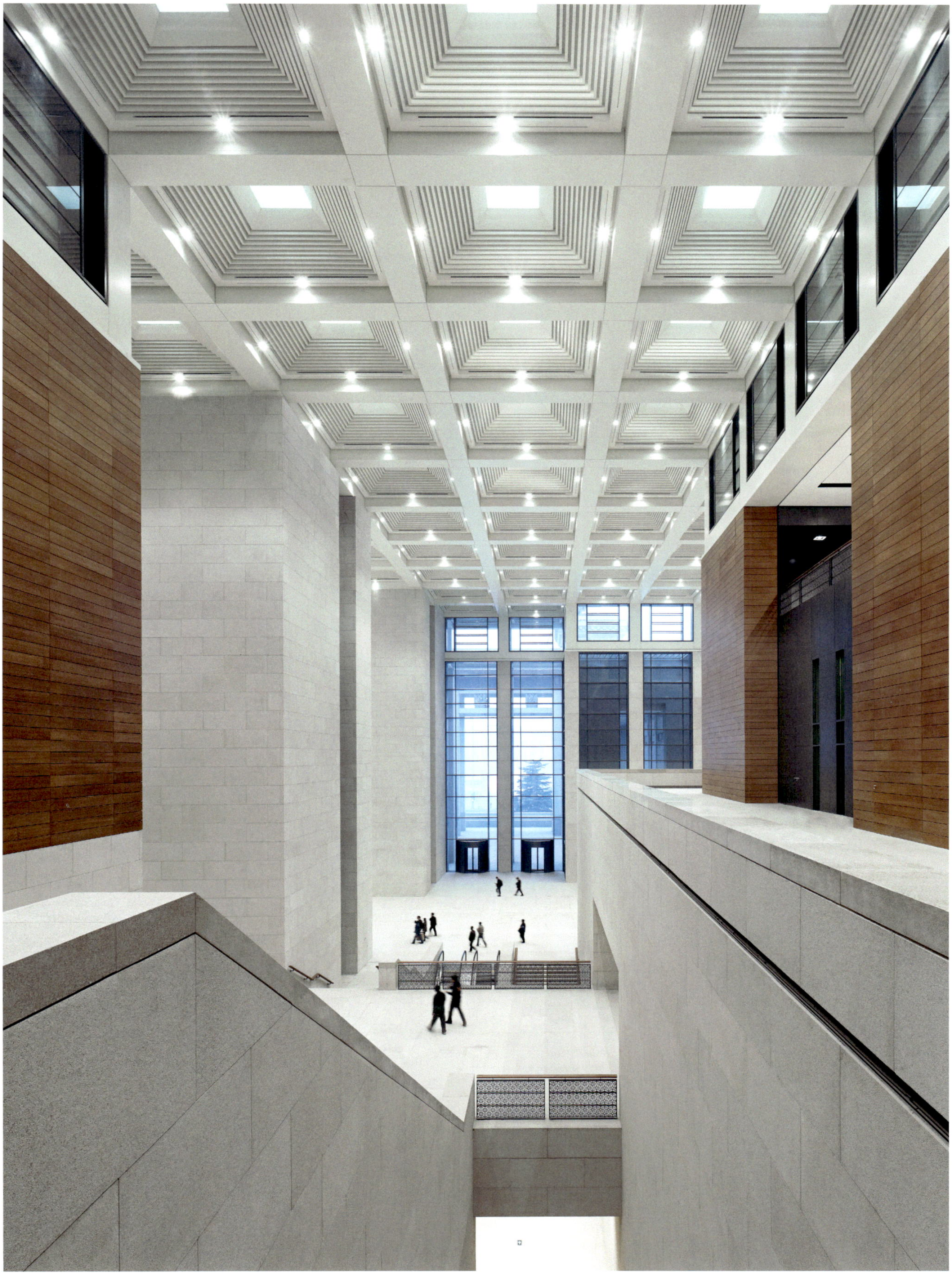

Hinterleuchtete Gussglasplatten aus Recyclingmaterial charakterisieren die Jade-Halle oberhalb des Forums.
The Jade Hall above the Forum is notable for its backlit cast glass plates made of recycled material.

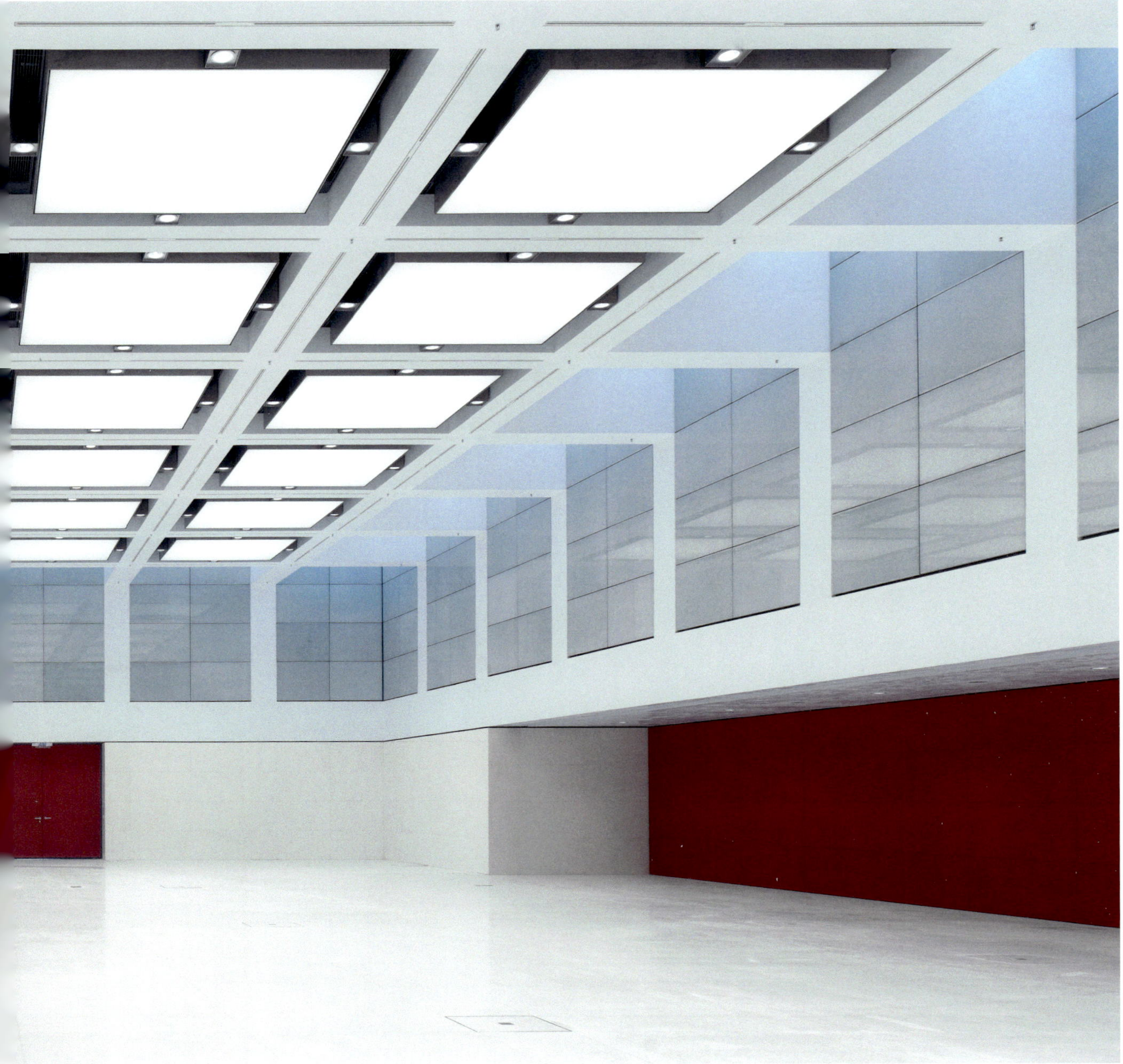

DAS CHINESISCHE NATIONALMUSEUM   Fotografische Dokumentation

↑ Neben hellem chinesischem Granitstein wurde in den Innenräumen Kirschholzwandverkleidung verwendet.
Aside from light Chinese granite stone, black cherry cladding was used inside the building.

↗ Die traditionelle chinesische Metallbaukunst lässt sich in den Eingangstüren und den Geländern wiederfinden.
The ornamentation of the entrance doors recurs in the forming of the balustrades in the interior of the museum.

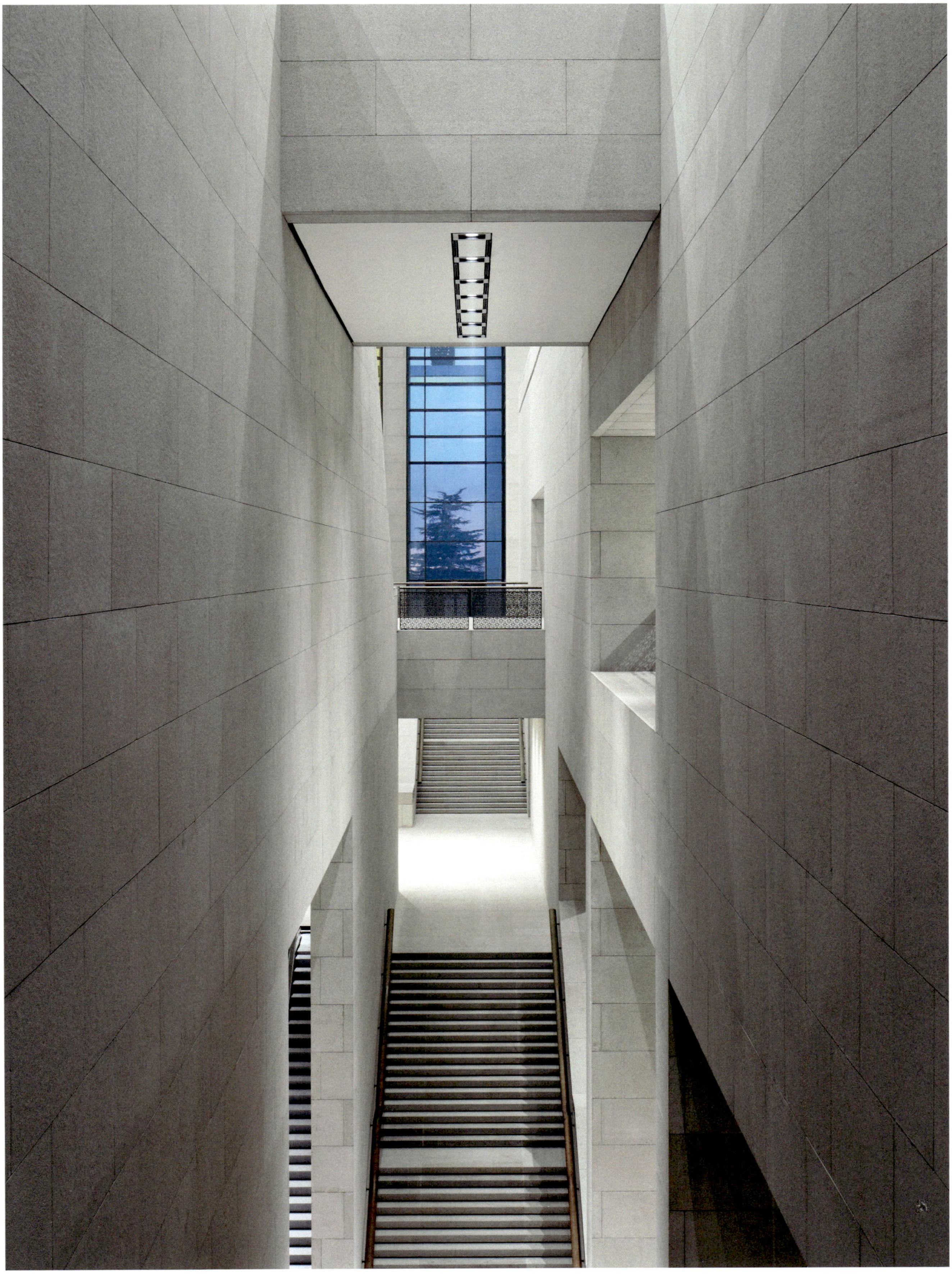

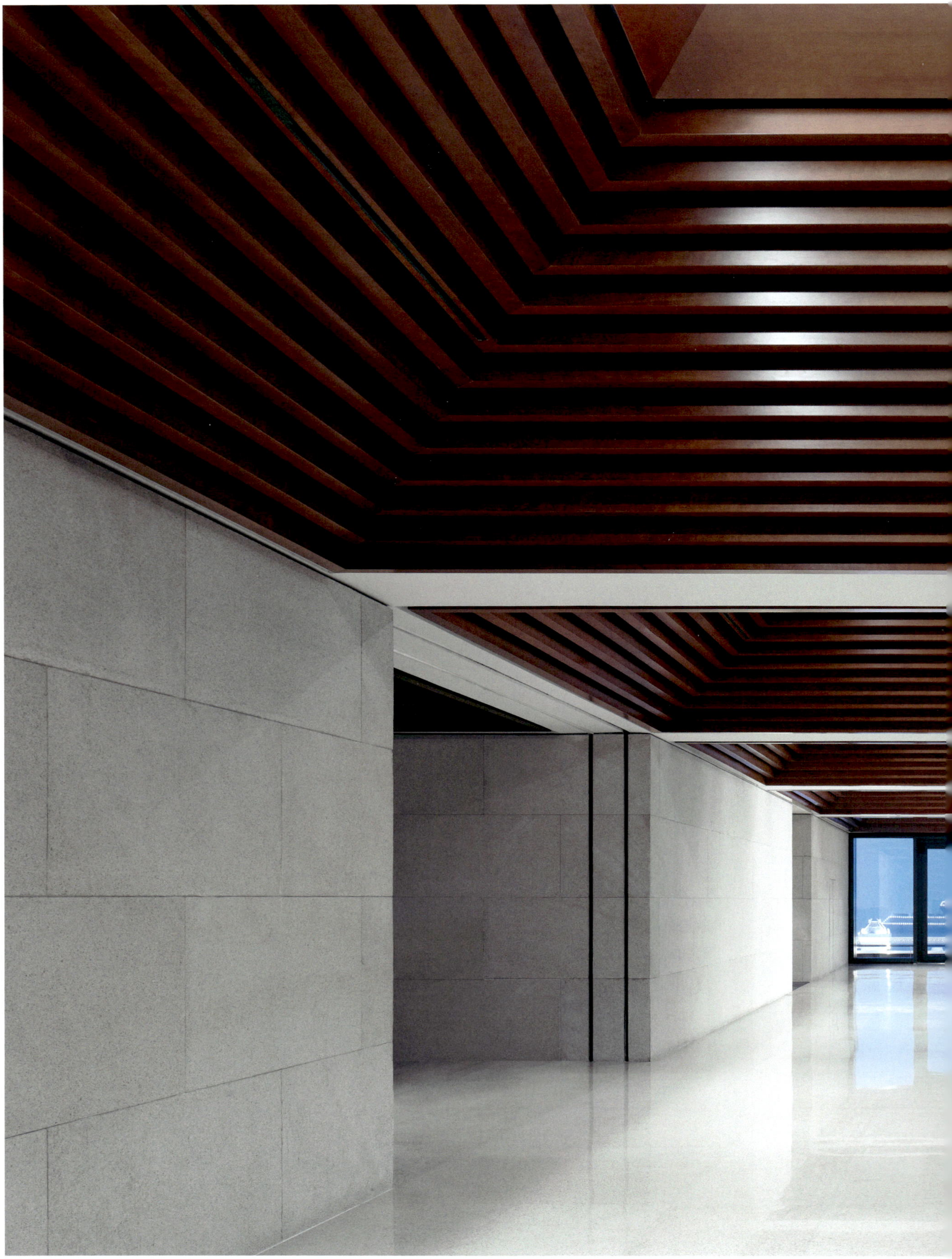

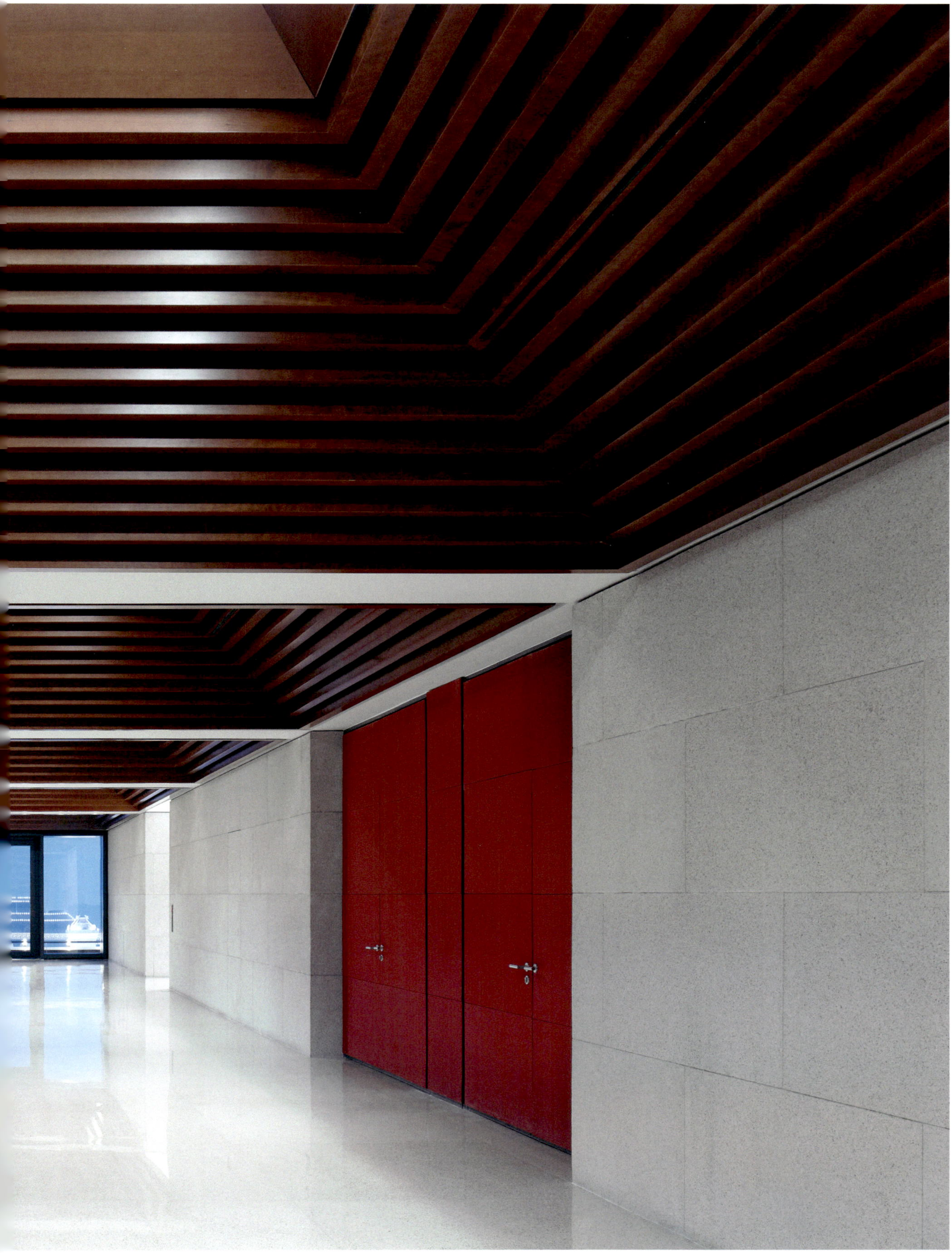

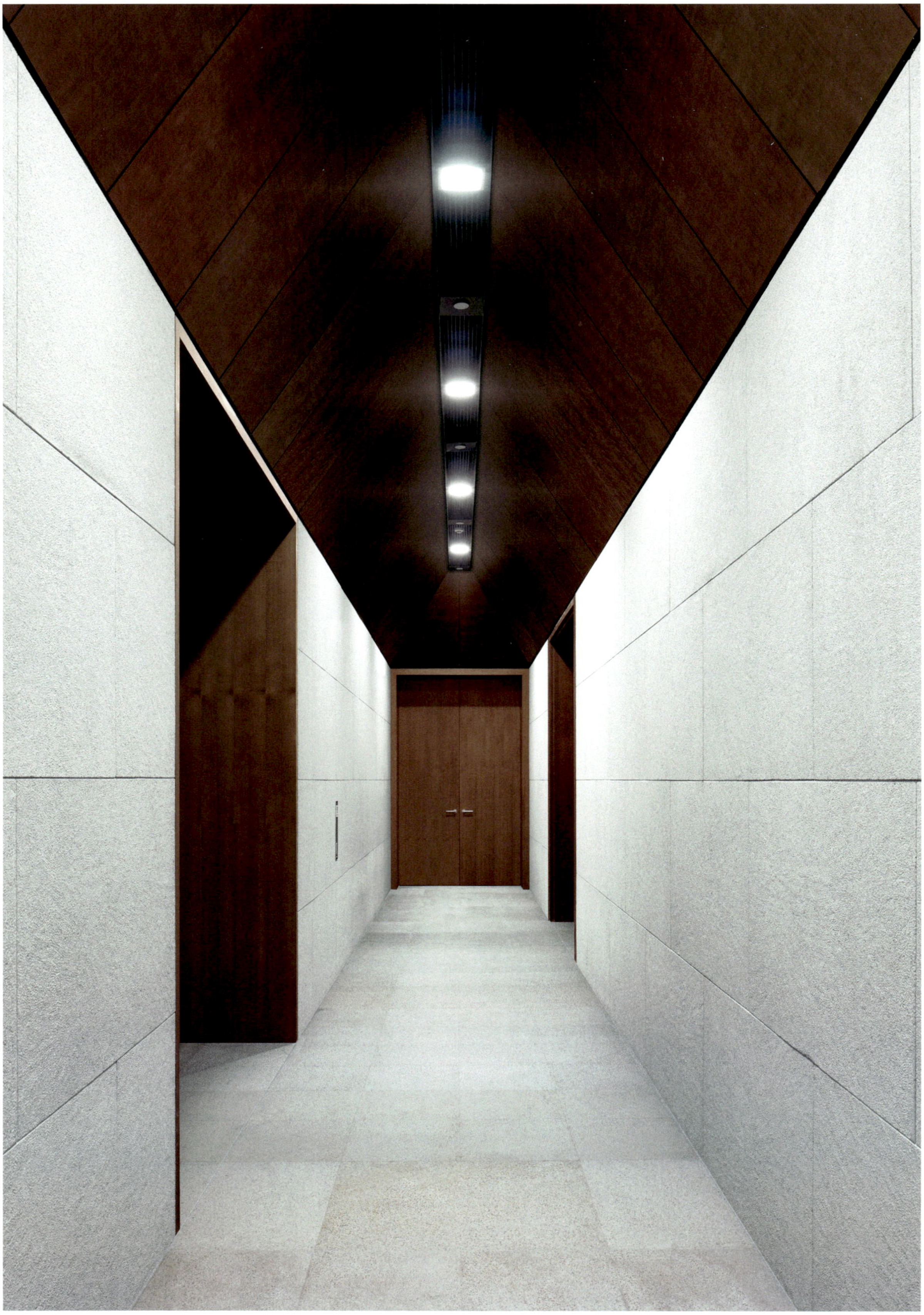

THE NATIONAL MUSEUM OF CHINA   Photographic Documentation

← 🔲 Korridor mit Zugang
zur Dachterrasse und
Jade-Halle
Corridor with access
to the Roof Terrace and
Jade Hall

← Korridor mit den
Zugängen zu den VIP-
Empfangsräumen
Corridor to the VIP
Reception Rooms

↑ Hauptspeiseraum im
VIP-Bereich nahe der
Dachterrasse
Main Dining Room in the
VIP area close to the Roof
Terrace

↑ Unterhalb der zentralen Halle befindet sich ein Auditorium mit 264 Sitzplätzen.
The auditorium below the Central Hall offers 264 seats.

↑ Das Theater hat 714 Sitzplätze
　The theater has 714 seats.

Lobbybereich beim Osteingang für
Auditorium und Theater
The lobby area for the Auditorium and
Theater at the eastern entrance

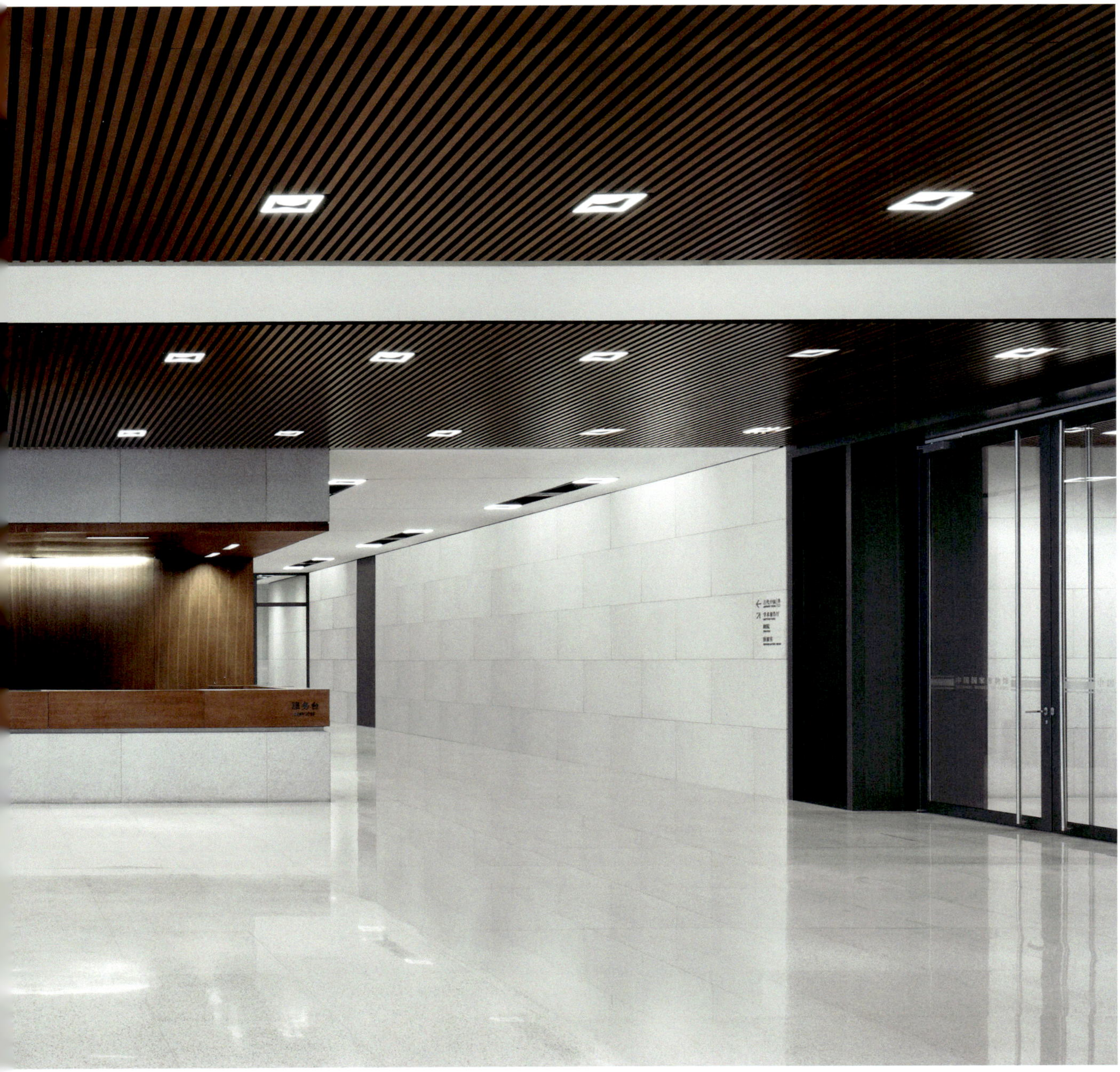

↑ Auch im Lesebereich der Bibliothek wurde
die Wand mit Kirschholz verkleidet.
Also in the reading area of the library, the walls
were clad with black cherry wood.

→ Bibliothek im Altbau
Library in the old building

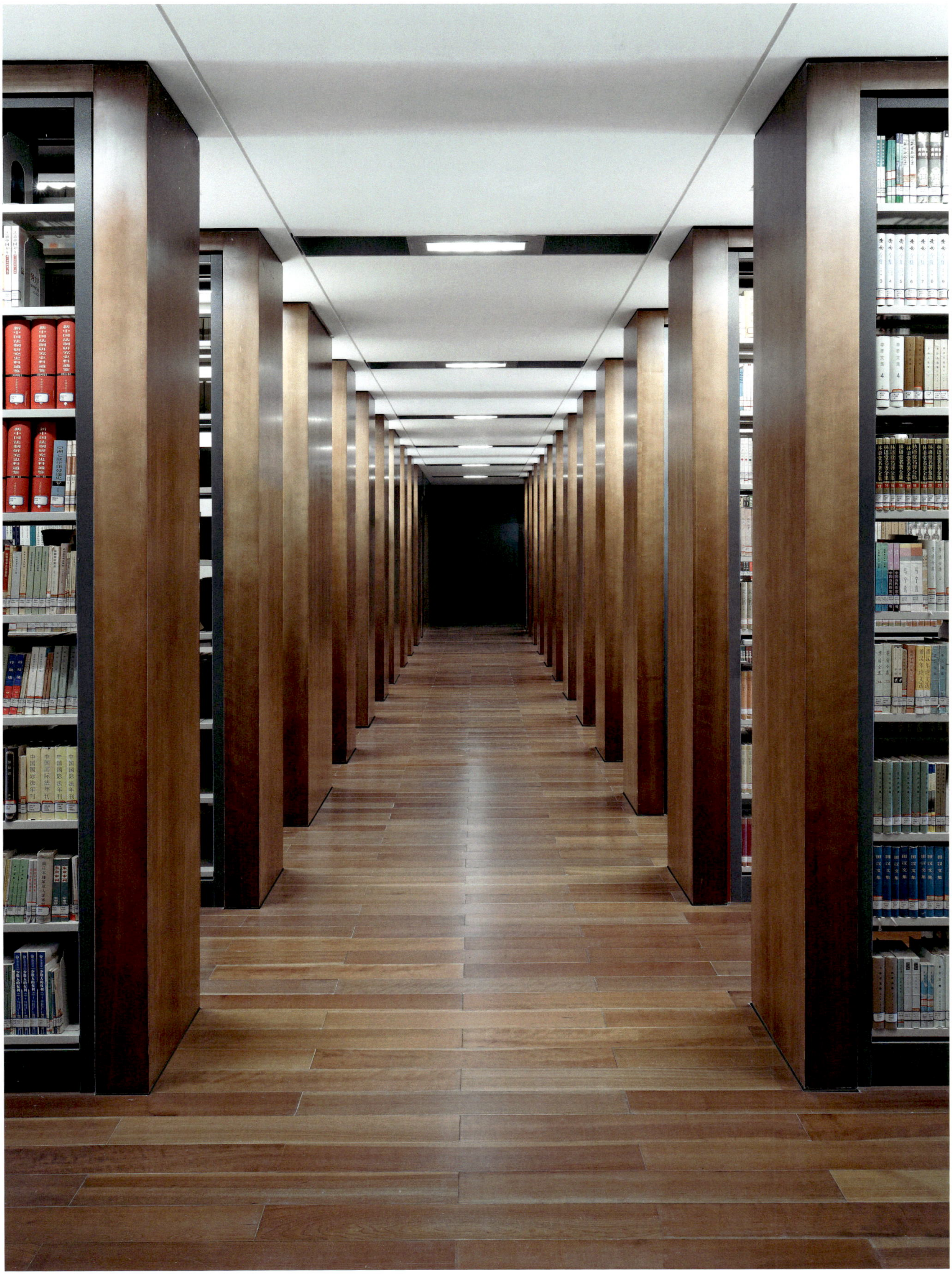

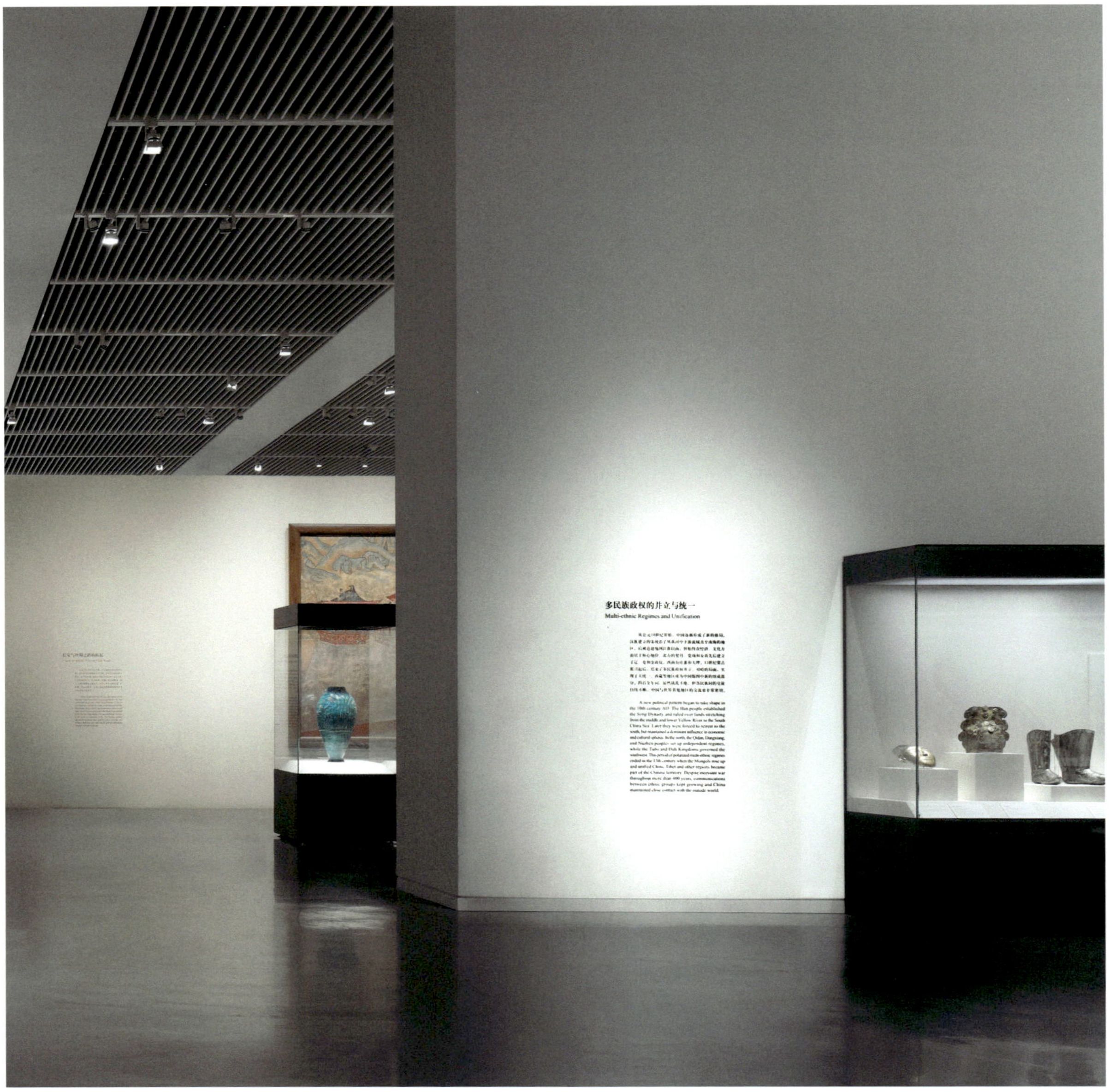
多民族政权的并立与统一
Multi-ethnic Regimes and Unification

THE NATIONAL MUSEUM OF CHINA Photographic Documentation

↖ ↑ Ausstellungsbereich ‚Historisches China' im Untergeschoss
'Ancient China' exhibition space in the basement

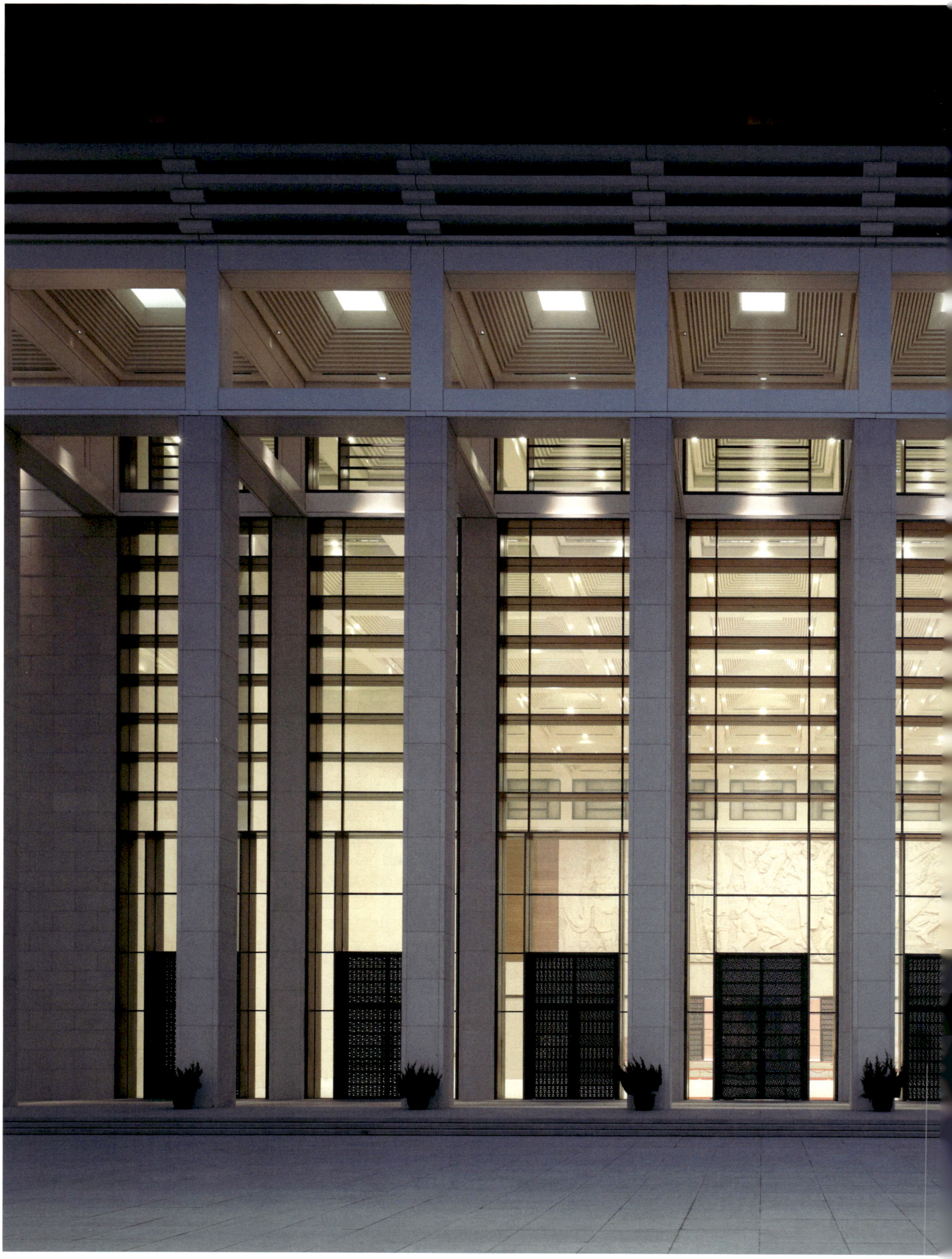

Eingang Westseite
Western entrance

Anhang

Appendix

Entwurfsteam Design team   gmp

Meinhard von Gerkan
Prof. Dr. h. c. mult. Dipl.-Ing. Architekt BDA

Gründungspartner, geboren 1935 in Riga/Lettland, 1965 Gründungspartner des Architekturbüros von Gerkan, Marg und Partner zusammen mit Volkwin Marg, 1974 Berufung an die TU Carolo-Wilhelmina zu Braunschweig als ordentlicher Professor/Lehrstuhl A für Entwerfen und Institutsleiter des Instituts für Baugestaltung A, Mitglied Freie Akademie der Künste zu Hamburg, 2005 Verleihung der Ehrendoktorwürde für Entwerfen durch die Chung Yuan Christian University in Chung Li/Taiwan, 2007 Verleihung der Ehrenprofessur durch das East China Normal University College of Design, Shanghai/China, 2007 Präsident der Academy for Architectural Culture (aac), zahlreiche Auszeichnungen, u. a. Fritz Schumacher Preis, Rumänischer Staatspreis, Plakette der Freien Akademie der Künste Hamburg, Großer Preis des Bundes Deutscher Architekten, Verleihung des Bundesverdienstkreuzes.

Founding partner, born 1935 in Riga/Latvia; 1965 co-founder with Volkwin Marg of the architectural partnership of von Gerkan, Marg and Partners; 1974 appointed professor, chair A for Design at the Carolo-Wilhelmina Technical University in Brunswick, head of Institute A for Architectural Design, member of the Freie Akademie der Künste in Hamburg; 2005 honorary doctorate in design from Chung Yuan Christian University in Chung Li/Taiwan; 2007 honorary professor, East China Normal University College of Design, Shanghai/China, 2007 president of the Academy for Architectural Culture (aac). Numerous awards, including Fritz Schumacher Prize, Romanian State Prize, bronze plaque of the Freie Akademie der Künste, Hamburg, BDA Prize, Federal Cross of Merit.

Stephan Schütz
Dipl.-Ing. Architekt BDA

Partner, geb. 1966 in Duisburg, seit 2006 Partner im Büro von Gerkan, Marg und Partner, Leitung der gmp-Büros Berlin, Peking, Shenzhen, Projekte u.a. Weimarhalle, Tempodrom, Berlin, Christliche Kirche, Peking, CYTS Plaza, Peking, Opernhaus Qingdao, Chinesisches Nationalmuseum, Peking, Sportzentrum Shenzhen.

Partner, born 1966 in Duisburg, graduate architect; partner at von Gerkan, Marg and Partners since 2006; management of the gmp offices in Berlin, Beijing and Shenzhen; projects include New Weimar Hall, New Tempodrom, Berlin, Christian Church, Beijing, CYTS Plaza, Beijing, Qingdao Grand Theater, National Museum of China, Beijing, Shenzhen Universiade Sports Center.

gmp

Doris Schäffler
Dipl.-Ing. Architektin BDA

Freie Architektin in Berlin, geboren 1967 in München, 1994 Diplom mit Auszeichnung an der TU Braunschweig, seit 1994 im Büro von Gerkan, Marg und Partner Berlin, 2000–2004 Büroleitung gmp Peking, seit 2009 eigenes Büro in Berlin. Projekte u.a. Restaurant VAU, Renaissance der Bahnhöfe, Weimarhalle, KPM, CYTS, Tianjin Biotech, Sommerhaus Diensdorf (ausgezeichnet mit dem Deutschen Holzbaupreis), Wohnhaus Berlin-Grunewald, Umbau 1930er-Jahre-Villa, Berlin-Ruhleben

Freelance architect in Berlin, born 1967 in Munich; diploma with distinction from Braunschweig Technical University 1994; working for von Gerkan, Marg and Partners Berlin since 1994, from 2000 to 2004 in charge of gmp Peking, own practice in Berlin since 2009. Projects include Restaurant VAU, "Renaissance of railway stations," Weimarhalle, KPM, CYTS, Tianjin Biotech, Diensdorf Summer House (received German Timber Construction award), residence Berlin-Grunewald, conversion of 1930s style villa Berlin-Ruhleben

Stephan Rewolle
Dipl.-Ing. Architekt

Assoziierter Partner, geboren 1967 in Skive/Dänemark, seit 2010 assoziierter Partner im Büro von Gerkan, Marg und Partner, Leitung des gmp-Büros Peking, Projektleitungen u. a. Chinesisches Nationalmuseum, Peking, Bahnhof Tianjin West, TV Station, Guangzhou.

Associate partner, born Skive/Denmark 1967; graduate architect, associate partner at von Gerkan, Marg and Partners since 2010; management of gmp's Beijing office; project management of Chinese National Museum/Beijing, Tianjin West railway station, TV Station/Guangzhou etc.

gmp Partner China

Wu Wei
Dipl. Architekt ETH

Partner für China – geboren 1971 in Lanzhou/Gansu, China, 1992 Abschluss des Architektustudiums in Chongqing, China. Von 1992–1994 Architekt am Gansu Institute of Architectural Design, 1994–1995 Studium der Deutschen Sprache in der Schweiz, 1995–1997 Architekturstudium ETH Zürich und 1997–2000 Mitarbeit im Büro Skyline Architecture und in der Firma SwissGerman Consulting in Zürich, 2000 Diplom an der ETH Zürich am Lehrstuhl Prof. Mario Campi, seit 2000 Mitarbeit im Büro von Gerkan, Marg und Partner Architekten, seit 2001 Chefrepräsentant der gmp-Büros in Peking und Shanghai, seit 2004 assoziierter Partner im Büro von Gerkan, Marg und Partner, seit 2009 Partner für China im Büro von Gerkan, Marg und Partner.

Partner for China, born 1971 in Lanzhou/Gansu, China; completed architectural studies in Chongqing, China, in 1992. From 1992 to 1994 architect at the Gansu Institute of Architectural Design, 1994 to 1995 German language studies in Switzerland, 1995 to 1997 studied architecture at the ETH Zurich and from 1997 to 2000 worked for Skyline Architecture and SwissGerman Consulting in Zurich; qualified at ETH Zurich (Prof. Mario Campi) in 2000, since then work for von Gerkan, Marg and Partners, Architects (gmp); since 2001 chief representative of gmp's offices in Beijing and Shanghai, since 2004 Associate Partner with von Gerkan, Marg and Partners and since 2009 Partner at gmp with responsibility for China.

Partnerbüro Partner Practice   CABR

Ma Lidong
Architect MA

1969 in Peking geboren, studierte an der School of Architecture, Tsinghua Universität, Masterabschluss. Stellvertretender Chefarchitekt bei CABR, Direktor des Architectural Design Institute
Wichtige Projekte: Peking Sunflower Tower; Kuwaitische Botschaft, China; SOHO Shang-Du Complex, Peking; Chinesisches Zentrum für Kontrolle und Prävention von Krankheiten; Chinesisches Nationalmuseum.

Born in 1969 in Beijing, graduated from the School of Architecture of Tsinghua University, Master degree. Deputy Chief Architect of China Academy of Building Research (CABR), the Director of the Architectural Design Institute of CABR; Projects include the Beijing Sunflower Tower, the Kuwait Embassy in China, the SOHO Shang-Du Complex Beijing, Chinese Center for Disease Control and Prevention, and the National Museum of China.

Wang Shuang
Architect

Geboren 1968 in Peking. Eingetragene Architektin. Abschluss 1992 an der School of Architecture, Tsinghua Universität, China. Stellvertretende Chefarchitektin bei ADI, CABR;
Wichtige Projekte: International School WEB; Bank of China (Hauptsitz Peking); Sanierung des Ministeriums für Bau; Indische Botschaft, Peking; DreamPort von CRLand, Peking; Chinesisches Nationalmuseum; Zhuhai Museum; Damei Plaza.

Born 1968 in Beijing. 1st Class Registered Architect. Graduated 1992 from School of Architecture, Tsinghua University. Deputy Chief Architect of ADI, CABR; Project includes: International School WEB; Bank of China headquater Bejing; Office Building Renovation Ministry of Construction; Embassy of India, Beijing; Dreamport of C.R.Land, Beijing; National Museum of China; Zhuhai Museum; Damei Plaza.

Projektleitung Project Management

gmp

Matthias Wiegelmann
Dipl.-Ing. Architekt (FH)

Geboren 1969 in Worms/Deutschland, seit 2010 Direktor im Büro von Gerkan, Marg und Partner, Mitarbeiter des gmp-Büros Peking, Projektleitungen u. a. Chinesisches Nationalmuseum, Peking, Bund SOHO, Schanghai, Fuxinglu SOHO, Schanghai, National Exhibition Center, Tianjin

Born 1969 in Worms/Germany. Director at von Gerkan, Marg and Partners since 2010, member of gmp Peking office; project management includes: Chinese National Museum, Peking; Shanghai SOHO Bund; Shanghai SOHO Fuxinglu; National Exhibition Centre, Tianjin.

Patrick Pfleiderer
Dipl.-Ing. Architekt

Geboren 1967 in Tübingen/Deutschland, seit 2012 Assoziierter Direktor im Büro von Gerkan, Marg und Partner, 2005–12 Mitarbeiter des gmp-Büros Peking, Projektleitungen u. a. Chinesisches Nationalmuseum (Ausführung), Peking; Huai An International Exhibition Center, Jiangsu Provinz; Trendy International, Guangzhou.

Born 1967 in Tübingen/Germany, Associate Director at von Gerkan, Marg and Partners since 2012, member of gmp Peking office from 2005 to 2012, project management includes: Chinese National Museum Peking (execution), Huai An International Exhibition Centre, Jiangsu Province, Trendy International, Guangzhou.

Autoren und Fotografen Authors and Photographers

Lu Zhangshen

1955 geboren. Direktor des Chinesischen Nationalmuseums, stellvertretender Vorsitzender der China International Culture Association, Direktor der China Calligraphers Association, besonderer Wissenschaftler der chinesischen Akademie der Kalligraphie und Berater der China International Association of Calligraphy and Painting und der China Association of Collectors.
Lus kalligraphische Werke wurden in diversen Zeitungen und Zeitschriften veröffentlicht, und sind Teil von Museums- und Gedenkhallensammlungen. Weitere Veröffentlichungen u. a.: Collection of "Lu Zhangshen's Calligraphy (2005)" und "Lu Zhangshen's Calligraphy Works (Juli 2007)".

Born in December, 1955. Director of the National Museum of China. Vice Chairman of the China International Culture Association, Director of the China Calligraphers Association, special researcher with the Chinese Academy of Calligraphy and consultant to the China International Association of Calligraphy and Painting, and the China Association of Collectors. Lu's works of calligraphy have been published in newspapers and magazines, and are part of museum and memorial hall collections. Other publications include: Collection of "Lu Zhangshen's Calligraphy (2005)" and Collection of "Lu Zhangshen's Calligraphy Works (July 2007)".

Prof. Dr. Martin Roth

Geboren 1955 in Stuttgart, Promotion an der Eberhard-Karls-Universität in Tübingen mit einer Dissertation über die Geschichte des kulturhistorischen Museums. 1987 – 88 Forschungsaufenthalt an der Maison des Sciences de l'Homme und am Deutschen Historischen Institut in Paris, u.a. zur Geschichte und Ausstellungspraxis von Weltausstellungen und Museen. 1991 bis 2000 Leiter des Deutschen Hygiene-Museums, Dresden. 1996 bis 2001 verantwortlich im Management der EXPO 2000 für den Themenpark, die Weltweiten Projekte und den Global Dialogue bei der EXPO 2000 GmbH, Hannover. 1995–2003 Präsident des Deutschen Museumsbundes, Berlin. Seit 2003 Honorarprofessur für Kulturpolitik und Kulturmanagement an der TU Dresden. 2001–11 Generaldirektor der Staatlichen Kunstsammlungen in Dresden und seit 2011 Direktor des Viktoria and Albert Museums in London.

Born 1955 in Stuttgart, awarded doctorate by Eberhard-Karls University in Tübingen for his dissertation on the history of museums and cultural politics. 1987 to 88, researcher at the Maison des Sciences de l'Homme and the Institute of German History in Paris on the history and practice of world exhibitions and museums, amongst other subjects. 1991 to 2000, curator of the German Hygiene Museum, Dresden. 1996 to 2001, member of EXPO 2000 management, with responsibility for thematic exhibitions, international projects, and global dialogue at EXPO 2000 GmbH, Hanover. 1995 to 2003, President of the German Museums Association, Berlin. Since 2003, honorary professor for cultural policy and management at Dresden Technical University. 2001 to 2011, Director General of State Art Collections in Dresden and since 2011, Director of the Victoria and Albert Museum in London.

Dr. András Szántó
Autor und Journalist Author and Journalist

Beitragender Redakteur der Zeitschrift „The Art Newspaper" und Mitbegründer von „ArtworldSalon". Seine Beiträge sind in der „The New York Times", sowie in „Artforum", „Museum Practice" und anderen Veröffentlichungen erschienen. Er hat am Sotheby"s Institute of Art, N.Y. Vorträge über „Kunstbusiness" und „Kunstmarketing" gehalten und war Direktor des National Arts Journalism Program und des NEA Arts Journalism Institute an der Universtät in Columbia. Er berät führende Museen, Stiftungen und Unternehmen auf globaler Ebene. Er moderiert regelmäßig in der Serie „Art Basel Conversations".

Contributing editor for "The Art Newspaper" and co-founder of "ArtworldSalon". His writings have appeared in "The New York Times", "Artforum", "Museum Practice", and other publications. He has lectured in art business and art marketing at the Sotheby's Institute of Art, N.Y., and has been the director of the National Arts Journalism Program and the NEA Arts Journalism Institute at Columbia University. As a consultant, he advises leading museums, foundations, and corporations worldwide. He is a regular moderator of the Art Basel Conversations series.

Christian Gahl
Fotograf Photographer

geboren 1966 in München. 1993–1996 Studium der Architektur. Seit 1996 selbstständiger Architekturfotograf, international tätig u.a. für Architekturbüros Hild + K., Toyo Ito, Murphy/Jahn, Rem Koolhaas, HG Merz. Auch Künstler wie Keith Sonnier, Ulrich Rückriem, Walter de Maria oder Institutionen wie das Guggenheim New York, MoMA New York und die Neue Nationalgalerie Berlin zählen zu seinen Auftraggebern. Publiziert werden seine Bilder u.a. in „The Architectural Review", „A+U", „domus", „Neue Zürcher Zeitung".

Born in Munich in 1966. Studied architecture from 1993 to 1996. Freelance architectural photographer with international commissions for architects Hild + K., Toyo Ito, Murphy/Jahn, Rem Koolhaas, and HG Merz since 1996. His clients also include artists such as Keith Sonnier, Ulrich Rückriem, Walter de Maria, and institutions such as the Guggenheim New York, the MoMA New York, and the new National Gallery in Berlin. His photographs are published in such publications as "The Architectural Review", "A+U", "domus" and "Neue Zürcher Zeitung".

Prof. Zhou Rong

Geboren 1968, Masterabschluss Schwerpunkt Design an der Harvard University, Doktor der Architektur, Universität Tsinghua, Professor, stellvertretender Direktor des Magazins „World Architecture", renommierter Architekturkritiker

Born in 1968, graduated from Havard University with an MA in design, Doctor of architecture from Tsinghua University. Vice Professor, Vice chief director of the magazine "World Architecture", renowned architectural critic.

Projektdaten Project Data

Bauherr Client
The National Museum of China

Entwurf Wettbewerb Competition Design
Meinhard von Gerkan und and Stephan Schütz
mit with Stephan Rewolle und Doris Schäffler

Entwurf Realisierung Executed Design
Meinhard von Gerkan und and Stephan Schütz
mit with Stephan Rewolle

Mitarbeiter Entwurf Design Staff
Gregor Hoheisel, Katrin Kanus, Ralf Sieber, Du Peng,
Chunsong Dong

Projektleitung Realisierung Proj. Leaders Execution
Matthias Wiegelmann mit with Patrick Pfleiderer

Mitarbeiter Staff
Bao Wei, Johanna Enzinger, Anna Bulanda-J., Kong
Jing, Andreas Goetze, Guo Fuhui, Mulyanto, Chen
Yue, Zheng Xin, Gao Hua, Xing Jiuzhou, Helga
Reimund, Tobias Keyl, Christian Dorndorf, Annette
Loeber, Verena Fischbach, Jiang LinLin, Liu Yan,
Mehrafarin Ruzbehi, Yoko Uraji, Lu Han, Xia Lin, Tian
Jinghai, Uli Bachmann, Ajda Guelbahar, Iris Belle,
Sabine Stage

Projektleitung Project Leaders
Matthias Wiegelmann mit with Patrick Pfleiderer

Chinesisches Partnerbüro Chinese Partner Practice
CABR (Chinese Academy of Building Research),
Peking – Ma Lidong, Wang Shuang

Statik Structural Engineering
CABR, Peking

Elektrotechnik Electronic Engineering
CABR, Peking

Landschaftsdesign Landscaping
RLA Rehwaldt Landscape Architects, Dresden / Peking

Eventtechnologie Event Technology
ADA Acoustic Design Ahnert, Berlin

Lichtdesign Lighting Design
conceptlicht GmbH, Traunreut; Urban Planning Design
& Research Institute of Tsinghua University, Peking

Fassade Façade SuP Ingenieure GmbH,
Darmstadt/Peking

Akustik Acoustics Müller-BBM Group/
ADA Acoustic Design Ahnert

Projektmanagement Project Management
Beijing Guojin Consultants Co., Ltd., Peking

BGF GFA 192 000 m²

Planungsbeginn Initial Planning
2004

Umplanung Replanning
2005

Bildnachweis Picture Credits

Christian Gahl
Titelmotiv Cover + Seiten Pages 6–7, 22, 33–34, 64–95

gmp Archive
Pläne und Zeichnungen
Plans and Drawings
Seiten Pages 26–27, 30–31, 48–61

Yuan Ying
Visualisierungen
Visualizations
Seiten Pages 27 unten bottom, 28–29

ullstein bild
sinopictures/wenxiao
Seite Page 23

Boros Media
Plakat zur Ausstellung:
„Die Kunst der Aufklärung"
"The Art of the Enlightenment"
Seite Page 25

Keith Levit/Design Pics/Corbis
Seite Page 34 oben top

www.tieba.baidu.com
Seite Page 35

National Museum of China
Li Jing Bo
Seite Page 36

ON Grafik – Hamburg
modifizierte Welt- und Chinakarte,
Karte Peking Innenstadt
modified World and China Map,
Map Beijing Inner City
Seiten Pages 8–9, 11

Impressum Imprint

Konzept Concept
Michael Kuhn gmp
Leiter PR und Kommunikation Head of PR

Herausgeber Editors
Meinhard von Gerkan gmp
Stephan Schütz gmp
Ma Lidong CABR

Koordination Editorial Direction
Claudia Tiesler gmp
Xiaoshi Fang gmp
Shan Shan Zheng, Peking gmp

Layoutkonzept und Satz Layout and Typesetting
ON Grafik, Tom Wibberenz mit with
Hendrik Sichler, Hamburg

Lektorat Proofreading
Philipp Sperrle (de.)
Inez Templeton (engl.)

Übersetzung Translation
Hartwin Busch, Ashdon, UK (en.)
Christian Brensing, Berlin (de.),

Bildredaktion und -bearbeitung Picture Editing
Trixi Hansen gmp
Guido Brixner gmp

Reproduktion Reproduction
DZA Druckerei zu Altenburg GmbH

Druck und Bindung Print Production and Binding
DZA Druckerei zu Altenburg GmbH

Papier Paper
Multi Art Silk von by Papyrus Europe
150 g/m²

Schrift Font
Linotype Avenir Next Pro

© 2013 by jovis Verlag GmbH und and
gmp · Architekten von Gerkan, Marg und Partner

Das Copyright für die Texte liegt bei den Autoren. Das Copyright für die Abbildungen liegt bei den Fotografen/Inhabern der Bildrechte. Text by kind permission of the authors. Pictures by kind permission of the photographers/holders of the picture rights.

Alle Rechte vorbehalten.
All rights reserved.
Titelmotiv Cover Picture Christian Gahl
Bibliografische Information der Deutschen Nationalbibliothek
Bibliographic information published by the Deutsche Nationalbibliothek
Die Deutsche Nationalbibliothek verzeichnet diese Publikation in der Deutschen Nationalbibliografie;detaillierte bibliografische Daten sind im Internet über http://dnb.d-nb.de abrufbar.
The Deutsche Nationalbibliothek lists this publication in the Deutsche Nationalbibliografie; detailed bibliographic data are available on the internet at http://dnb.d-nb.de

jovis Verlag GmbH
Kurfürstenstraße 15/16
10785 Berlin

www.jovis.de

ISBN 978-3-86859-320-4